THE
BOOK
OF
NUGGETS

THE
BOOK
OF
NUGGETS

Compiled by Juliet Solomon

First published in Great Britain in 2023
by GoodKind Publishing

Copyright © Juliet Solomon 2023

All rights reserved. No part of this publication
may be reproduced, stored in a retrieval system, or
transmitted, in any form or by any means, electronic,
mechanical, photocopying, recording or otherwise
without the prior permission in writing of the
publisher and copyright owners.

The contents of this publication are believed correct
at the time of printing. Nevertheless the publisher
can accept no responsibility for errors or omissions,
changes in the detail given or for any expense or loss
thereby caused.

Every care has been taken to verify the contributions
in this book.

ISBN 978-1-3999-6844-7

1 3 5 7 9 10 8 6 4 2

Cover illustration by Jeff Fisher
Design and typography by Webb & Webb Design Ltd
Printed and bound in the UK

In Memory of my beloved Mum.

A real Lady.

Contents

Foreword
xi

Introduction
xiii

Contributions
1-229

Index of Contributors
230-241

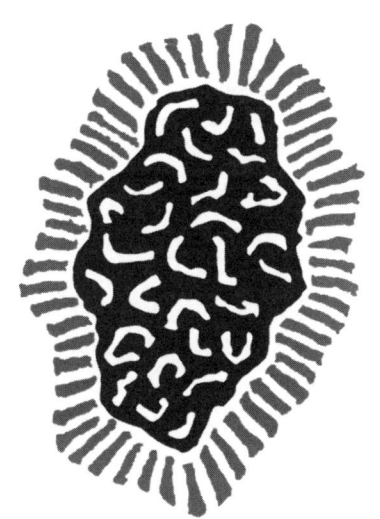

Foreword

When my dear Mum, Judith passed away from kidney disease I felt lost in so many ways.

There was of course the immediate, searing sense of grief which everyone feels when a much-loved parent leaves them. But after the initial shock, I wanted to find an appropriate way in which to honour Mum's memory and help others who suffer from kidney disease.

This book is the result.

I invited people to share nuggets of wisdom that they had collected along the way – that had helped them on their journey. I chose that as the theme of the book because it was deep in my Mum's nature to help people by sharing lessons from her own life. I saw how her kindness and thoughtfulness had touched so many lives, and I hoped that this book could do something to capture that spirit.

The response was truly humbling. Contributions poured in.

People gave so generously, selflessly, and warm-heartedly. They offered hard-won wise words mined from their own experience – and their notes are shot through with a rich, fascinating and enlightening blend of insight, intelligence, judgment, sanity, understanding and shrewdness. They are also by turns funny and serious; contemplative and quirky; surprising and painfully sad.

Nuggets came in from so many wonderful people, from every walk of life – many of them well-known; others less famous. But whatever their source, I was incredibly moved that so many good folk were willing to give of themselves and share valuable lessons from their own struggles, trials and joys.

I would like to say an enormous thank you to everyone who shared the wisdom they hold most dear.

I hope that this book will raise a significant amount of money for Kidney Research UK. Kidney disease is an area of medicine where we still have a lot to learn. Some advances have been made in treatment over the last few years. But there is so much more to do. If this book adds even a tiny amount to the work of the many brilliant and dedicated individuals who delve in these fields, I will be thrilled. It would be the perfect tribute to my Mum.

I would like to thank my hugely supportive family and friends for all their love. Also huge thanks to those who helped so enormously in collecting the nuggets: David Altschuler, Nicola Cobbold, Natalie Davidson, Gay Keogh, Alex Murphy, Dafna Spiro … The Zamet family – you have all been absolutely amazing. Also to Rebecca Jaks and Shosh Fenner for their immense kindness, to Webb & Webb Design Ltd for their brilliant work and to the Hope Agency for all their incredible help. I am deeply grateful.

I hope that you enjoy the book, and maybe/hopefully you will pick up some wisdom which helps you in your life.

Thank you.

Juliet Solomon
Compiler of 'The Book of Nuggets'

Introduction

Juliet's mother, Judith, died in 2021 as the result of a slowly progressive kidney condition. Subsequently she and her father, Sir Harry Solomon, decided to support Kidney Research UK, a major supporter of kidney research in the UK. That support took the form of a sizeable research grant to the charity, to be augmented with the proceeds from this 'Book of Nuggets', a highly original idea developed by the author. The initial grant is already being put to good use by doctors and scientists in various centres driving projects ranging from pure laboratory science to the best ways to support kidney patients and their families.

I had the privilege of looking after Judith during the last year of her life and was thus touched and flattered to be asked to write an introduction for this book that stands in her memory and it is to be hoped also to support through Kidney Research UK the national research effort in the field of kidney disease.

The 'nuggets' make fascinating reading, unsurprising given the remarkable collection of contributors Juliet has assembled from broad swathes of our society. Some will have had first-hand experience of kidney disease while many more will have had more indirect contact through family and friends – these diseases are much commoner than is generally appreciated. All have given their time generously in support of this project.

Professor Sir John Cunningham
Trustee, Kidney Research UK

> **Never take advice** from anyone who wants to give you advice!

Robert Carlyle OBE
Actor

Professor David Crystal OBE
Linguist and Writer

Nobody knows where the word nugget came from.

The Oxford English Dictionary first records it in the early 1800s in Ireland and Scotland, and also, somehow, Australia. It meant a small, stocky person or animal – especially one that was smaller than expected.

The notion caught on.

By the end of the century it was being used in Australia to talk about small lumps of precious metal found in the earth, in New Zealand to talk about small rocky outcrops in the sea, and everywhere to describe a small lump of anything – a nugget of sugar, cake, chocolate... Then, in the mid-twentieth century, the really famous one: nuggets of chicken!

An early Irish spelling of nodget suggests a pronunciation of the gg, to be like the consonant in judge. And indeed the word nudge is known in some nineteenth-century dialects in England to mean a lump, and knudge in Scotland for a short, sturdy person or animal. Maybe that's the origin.

It didn't take long for the sense to develop further, to mean any small valuable thing, especially one concealed in something larger, such as a nugget of great poetry within a collection. I wouldn't be surprised to see it being used to describe the items in a collection of wisdom pieces one day. And maybe its rare use as a verb too: to nugget.

If you're reading this, you've been nuggeting.

Stephen Fry
Writer, Actor, Comedian, Broadcaster

It's a very American characteristic for sophisticated minds to find surprisingly simple ways of expressing important insights. The philosopher Richard Rorty likes to say: "Don't scratch where it doesn't itch." An apparent counter to that comes from another deceptively homespun thinker, Mark Twain: "An uneasy conscience is a hair in the mouth." In the end it's not other people that are life's aggravation, it's the conscience, the Jiminy Cricket whispering to us that we are lacking, we have fallen short, we have done wrong. That's a hair in the mouth all right. But there again, we will so often scratch where we don't itch. Somewhere between the two is a key to a more contented life perhaps.

Simpler advice to follow was told me by a great food writer. Don't eat at a place with "Ma's" or "Famous" in its name. "Ma's Famous Fried Chicken" would be a double no. Don't eat at a restaurant that has a poster or cutout of an edible animal outside: a fish or pig with napkin round its neck looking hungry and brandishing a knife and fork. And don't go into an "Irish" pub that has a neon shamrock in the window.

Lord Franks, when he was British Ambassador in Washington, was rung up by a journalist and asked, since it was the season, what he hoped to get for Christmas. He was distraught to see the next day's paper with the following story. "Christmas Lists of the Embassies. The French Ambassador wants world peace. The German Ambassador wants an end to hunger. The British Ambassador wants a box of crystallised fruits."

Personally, I think Lord Franks was the heroic one. Keep your ambitions realistic and workable.

Sir Chris Bonington CBE
Mountaineer
Never be afraid to turn back, you don't have to get to the top to achieve, learn and enjoy. If conditions are against you, stopping and turning back or taking a different direction could save your life.

Ed O'Brien
Guitarist, Songwriter and member of the band Radiohead
THE JOURNEY IS EVERYTHING
The journey *really* is everything ... reaching the destination will obviously bring with it a certain amount of satisfaction, but the real prize is in how we get there ... How did we get on when things weren't so rosy? How did we conduct ourselves? How did/do we treat others? What did we really learn about ourselves in those situations where we were supremely challenged? *That* is the stuff

of life ... And here's the other thing... If you can also put love and kindness towards others and towards yourself at the very heart of your journey, then that appears to be the key to reaching your destination with a smile on your face and love in your heart.

Sir Michael Palin CBE
Actor, Writer, Broadcaster, Comedian and Television Presenter
Try and see as much of the world as you can. And I mean, really see it, not just from a safe distance.

Get stuck in. Enjoy the diversity, talk with the people, enjoy the differences. You'll have some adventures you never expected, some good, some bad, but you'll almost certainly see and do things you'll never forget.

And remember the more you travel the more you'll understand your own country.

Neil Hyman
Kidney transplant recipient
THE GIFT OF LIFE
Lying on the reclining chair in the dialysis unit. Staring at the crimson blood slowly winding its way through the multitude of tubes and back into my body, cleansed of toxins. Watching the clock slowly tick down 4.00, 3.59, 3.58... The monotony punctuated only by the nurses moving quietly and efficiently from patient to patient. Without masks or PPE as this is the early days of the pandemic. There are rumours that dialysis patients, in the extremely vulnerable category, are adding to the Government's daily statistics. Every visit to have our life saving treatment, the journey to and from, is potentially walking into the lion's den.

I turn to my right. A middle-aged man, younger than me. He has no suitable donor in the family or from within his friend group and has been on the waiting list for over 3 years. He goes to work each day, returns home exhausted to his wife and children, and spends his free time here in the hospital. He keeps going for himself, for his family. He closes his eyes and gently dozes. On my left an elderly lady, grey-haired, a tired and worn look, considered not healthy enough for a transplant. Dialysis for the rest of her life. She gazes up at the ceiling, blankly, without focus, as the minutes and hours go slowly by. And across the room, a young 18-year old. He has family that are willing to offer him a lifeline, but none of them are a match or healthy enough to be considered as a suitable donor. Yet he smiles, gestures hello, and chats animatedly to anyone who comes near. Each, in his or her own way, finds how to manage this intrusive, time-consuming, life-restricting affliction.

Where do I fit in with this eclectic group of people with a common illness, a shared sense of despondency, but with a collective will to get through?

Do you smoke, asked the consultant. No, I replied. Do you drink? Only very occasionally, I said. Do you exercise? All the time. Is there kidney disease in the family? No. You're unlucky then, concluded the doctor. It's a silent disease that can creep up on any of us, don't be fooled.

The shock of the diagnosis. Final stage renal failure. Immediate dialysis. No time for a fistula. A parachute patient, catheter in the chest, extra risk of infection. But different from many, I have the prospect of an early solution, a family donor, a transplant, hope. They just have to complete the final compatibility tests on my sister. And then Covid punctures that balloon of optimism. Lockdown is announced the day before the tests are due to take place. All tests are cancelled. Live donor transplant surgery is cancelled. A day turns into a month, into two, into half a year. And then as suddenly as the blanket of darkness was thrown over us, the light appears, tests and transplants recommence. The tests are successful. My mother frets at the end of the phone as two of her children are taken down to surgery at the same time, a parent's worst nightmare. I wake up. Sore, delirious, with a new kidney that is functioning beautifully inside me. My sister is also well, but because of Covid restrictions I can't see her, to have that silent moment with her, to look into her eyes, gaze upon her face, and thank her for the gift of life.

Aspirations, adventure and modernity put geographical distance between us. Politics, social issues and race, trans & gender views are creating conflict between us. Traditional family and community ties and support are being loosened. And yet in the darkest of times it is family and community that we turn to, who put their own lives on the line to save ours. I am one of the lucky ones, with a wife, children and family to surround me with love and support, and I want to tell the tale.

Sir Terry Waite
Humanitarian and Author

Many years of my life were spent negotiating for the release of hostages. Such work is both difficult and dangerous. One always has in the back of one's mind that one might well be captured or killed but these thoughts have to be controlled otherwise one would never engage in such work. I had many successes but eventually things went wrong and I was captured whilst attempting to negotiate for the release of hostages in Beirut.

I spent almost five years in solitary confinement when I was chained to the wall, slept on the floor and never saw or spoke with anyone for years. I had no books or papers for about four years and was often in the dark.

To be a successful negotiator one has to be able to listen and to build trust. If in any way trust is broken then one is in dire trouble.

The story is too long to relate here but suffice to say trust was broken between me and the kidnappers because of political duplicity. I went back to meet them in an attempt to rebuild the relationship.

We met, as usual, in total secrecy. In all my visits with them they had never allowed me to visit the hostages. They had provided proof of life but access to them was denied. On what proved to be my final meeting before being incarcerated they said that this time I could visit the hostages as one was seriously ill and about to die. I replied that if I went they would keep me. They said they would not. I asked for twenty-four hours to think about their proposal and they agreed to that.

In the next several hours I took advice from several quarters. Some said I ought to walk away now. Others were not sure and there were some who said that a promise had been made and would be kept.

I was dubious.

I would not like anyone reading this to think that I am full of altruism. I believe that when we do something for others, consciously or unconsciously, we are also doing something for ourselves. I thought that if the kidnappers were telling me the truth, and that hostage died and I had not taken the opportunity to visit him, I would have to live with my conscience for the remainder of my life. The next night I went to see them and was taken hostage myself.

Well, you might ask, where is the nugget in all of this?

I cannot and will not say that I have always done what I believe to be the right thing in life. I have often behaved blindly or selfishly, but there sometimes comes a time in life when you know that you have to do what you believe to be right almost regardless of the personal consequences. You have to be able to live with yourself.

Yes, the years spent alone were hard but they also proved to be a blessing. Prior to captivity I had always had sympathy for the poor and the outcast. Captivity changed that sympathy into empathy. Sympathy is to feel sorry. Empathy is to know in your very being what it is like to suffer and be regarded as worthless. Life is full of suffering and many people suffer through no fault of their own. However, often within suffering there are the seeds of something new and creative. I have found that.

Looking back perhaps I was rash or even reckless but from that experience many new opportunities have arisen.

It is my sincere hope that this book will stimulate many good and positive actions and show once again that suffering need not destroy.

Steven Brown
Paralympian, Television Presenter, Public Speaker and Athlete Mentor

I remember a bad day in hospital in 2005.

It wasn't long after the fall that damaged my spinal cord and left me needing a wheelchair for the rest of my life. At the time, it felt like life wasn't going well. I needed help dressing, washing and with other personal tasks—much more help than I wanted at the age of 24.

I remember being peckish, so I made my way in my wheelchair to get an apple.

I picked an apple from the bowl on the table and put it on my lap. As I turned to make my way back across the room, the apple fell and rolled under the bed. My emotions got the better of me, and I cried. Total, uncontrollable sobbing.

This was the second time I'd cried since my injury. The first was when I was measured for a wheelchair. There, at the top of the form, in black and white, it said "Steve Brown: Non-Walker." In that moment, the magnitude of my situation became apparent. I cried because it finally clicked – my disability meant I was never going to walk again.

This time I cried because I was starting to realise the limitations of my disability. It's much more than not being able to put one foot in front of the other. It's not being able to get your phone in the night. It's not being able to dress yourself. It's not being able to get an apple from under the bed.

In that moment, it felt like no one understood my frustrations. It was sinking in now: being paralysed had cost me my job, my lifestyle, my friendships, my sense of self-worth – and now it had cost me an apple. In that moment, looking at the apple under the bed, I felt so alone.

I felt the presence of someone at the door. I wiped my tears away to see Lou, the cleaner, standing with her mop. She was a happy soul and always brightened up the place, and I don't just mean with glass cleaner. Gently, she asked what was wrong. Sobbing, red-faced, full of embarrassment, I pulled myself together just long enough to sit up straight and explain that I'd dropped an apple. Now that I was saying it out loud, it sounded so silly.

I gathered myself together with a few deep breaths as Lou leant the mop against the wall. She walked straight past me without even a glance. She looked at the table, turned to me, now with a smile on her face, and simply said, "But you have three other apples here; what's the problem? Why not get another apple?"

That was the eureka moment. It has stayed with me as a life lesson. Why not get another apple?

At the time Lou meant it entirely literally, but now I use her words as a metaphor for how I make and shape my decisions. That moment taught me to pick my battles and helped me realise there are always other ways. If I'm willing to explore options and work hard to make opportunities, there is always something to be found.

This is about looking at situations purposefully, objectively and, most of all, with honesty. It means you can see when something is worth pursuing or if it's out of reach. Thinking critically will give you a chance to see what is available.

If an apple is out of reach, go back to the table and choose another from the bowl. Lou taught me that.

Sir David Jason
Actor
A little nugget of wisdom which has meant a lot to me is one voiced by Del Boy, a character I was fortunate enough to play for many years.

He often used to say, when faced with a challenge or opportunity, 'He who dares wins.'

Using this saying in my own life means that I would always have a go at something which was challenging or daunting because, unless an attempt was made, I would never know what I was capable of.

I always felt it was better to try and fail than not to try at all so that we don't spend our lives saying, 'If only...'

Sir Ray Davies
Musician; Lead Vocalist, Rhythm Guitarist and Songwriter for The Kinks
My friend Pete Quaife, the original Kinks bass player, passed away with kidney failure and I dedicated these words to him from the stage in Glastonbury:

> 'Thank you for the days
> Those endless days, those sacred days you gave me.'

Dame Maureen Lipman
Actor, Writer and Comedian
Start the day with a glass of hot water with lemon juice, cider

vinegar, a shake of cayenne pepper and a smidge of turmeric mixed with a drop of olive oil. Splash of maple syrup won't hurt. It sounds awful I know but it quickly becomes addictive.

You'll hate me but a cold bath, six inches, or shower is worth it for the glow afterwards. Wild swimming is not for me. Tangly dangly stuff – eurgh.

Would it kill you, ladies, to start the day with a few weight lifts for those Michelle Obama arms?

Rosa Mosqueta oil is the best ever facial oil.

Try Bottarga. It is the roe of a grey mullet and is incredible with lemon, oil, garlic and warm French loaf. Better still with spaghetti. Expensive but not like caviar, ruinous.

Over sixty? Consciously pick your feet up, and don't 'shlurry.' Your foot muscles have weakened somewhat over time.

Dance. Even alone is good.

Create a little thing daily. A cake, a drawing. The app Art Set is good for painting on your iPad. Oil, acrylic, pastel – it's all there. No brown pictures because you didn't wash your brushes. And no mess.

Herbamare is a mixture of herbs and veg you can use instead of salt. No preservatives and tastes scrummy.

Your radio is your friend. They can call it 'podcast' or Audible or whatever they want but it is still radio. You can walk with it, sleep with it, sing with it and it is mostly free.

Prepare questions and take notes at the doctor's. Type them up so they stick in your memory.

Listen and Learn from your grandchildren. They are wise as well as wonderful.

Take a brave stance against small injustices. Democracy is built into our DNA. Support it.

Don't panic if a name goes from your head. It comes back. Too late of course but trust it's in there still.

Read the Olive Kitteridge books by Elizabeth Strout.

Watch the film *Best In Show*.

Surround yourself with witty people. You need to laugh.

Watch *La Strada*. You need to cry.

Don't buy scarves for women over sixty. We are inundated. Moisturiser and mascara please. And we don't mind tokens.

Keep some coins in your bag. Beggars do so badly since cards are payment. It's only the price of a macchiato.

Don't go on and on.

I'm done.

Delia Smith CBE
Writer, Broadcaster and Cook

Don't be afraid to fail because if you are not afraid to fail you can do anything.

Alan Johnson
Writer and Politician

Given that Polonius was the principal counsellor to the King of Denmark, the quality of the wisdom he imparts to his son Laertes (according to Shakespeare in *Hamlet*) should come as no surprise.

The father worries about his son travelling abroad for the first time and fears that they'll be separated forever.

I've always found his advice to be timeless, as applicable to my actual life as to the fictional life of Laertes.

"Costly thy habit as thy purse can buy but expressed in fancy not gaudy; for the apparel oft proclaims the man" – sums up the attitude of us West London mods in the sixties determined to dress as smartly as anyone despite our lack of wealth.

"Neither a borrower nor a lender" be summed up the attitude of me and my first wife as we struggled to bring up our young family whilst avoiding the perils of HP (hire purchase).

"Give Everyman thy ear but few thy voice", should be the watchword of every politician.

But the most important nugget was saved for the peroration of this fatherly counsel.

"This above all," says Polonius, "to thine own self be true, and it must follow, as the night the day, thou canst not then be false to any man".

Sir Geoffrey Boycott
Retired English First Class Cricketer and Broadcaster

In autumn 2002 I was told I had a cancerous tumour on the left side of my tongue.

Being told you have cancer is everyone's nightmare because often it is a death sentence. My wife Rachael and I were discussing with the Professor what treatment options were open to me when he said, "if you do nothing I give you three months". In other words I would be dead just after Christmas. The first person to tell was our daughter.

It was Emma's fourteenth birthday on 5th September, so she came home that night from her grandma's house as we had organised a party for her the next day. She was also due to go back to her boarding school, after the long summer break, three days later. We had to explain to her that I did have cancer after all, and there were tears all round. It still breaks my heart just thinking about that moment. Having to tell this to my only child, especially at such a young age, is probably one of the hardest things I have ever had to do. It was all very distressing, and made me cry. I felt I had been given a death sentence.

Nowadays, I am not ashamed to admit it, but at the time I was embarrassed, ashamed and upset because over the next few days I would often go into a room on my own and break down in tears. A grown man crying, it was embarrassing, and I would try to hide it, even from Rachael. It was so distressing, my mind was in turmoil, and I could not think straight, my head was in a total spin. I was getting angry at myself because here I was breaking down all the time.

After a few days of this I had to tell myself, "Listen, crying ain't going to make you better. If you just sit in a corner and keep crying you sure as hell definitely are going to die." So I said to myself, "What are you going to do about it? Pick yourself up and give it your best shot. Whatever it takes, be positive. This is ridiculous: I have always had patience, concentration and been mentally strong with my batting."

To all those people who are unlucky to have awful illness all I would say to you is ... life is so precious so fight for it.

Sadiq Khan
Mayor of London

I'm proud to represent such a forward-looking, global city.

London today is one of the most diverse cities in the world. One in three Londoners was born outside the UK, more than 300 languages are spoken on our streets and every faith is freely practised.

I grew up on a housing estate in Tooting, south London, which is a great, diverse part of London. We were not that well-off, but my parents worked hard to build a better life for our family. My dad was a bus driver for many years and my mum was a seamstress.

London was very different back then and there was a lot more overt racism. When my parents first came to Britain, there were signs up where we lived that said: "No blacks, no Irish, no dogs". And, by black, they meant anyone who was not white.

When I was growing up there was a lot of unemployment and poverty, but I'm grateful for the opportunities I was given to get on in life – a home for our family, a good education, and the opportunities to succeed. My experiences shaped me and my political outlook in many ways – and my biggest motivation now as Mayor is to ensure that every young Londoner can get the opportunities to reach their potential that London gave to me and my family.

Today in London, on the whole, we don't just tolerate one another or just accept our differences, we respect and celebrate them. But we have to be honest and admit that we're far from perfect. Our communities have been changing rapidly and our sense of social cohesion is being put to the test like never before.

A lack of integration makes it harder for people from different backgrounds to understand each other. It can breed mistrust and anxiety and fuel the development of the politics of division. It's no good sticking our heads in the sand or acting as if this issue will simply sort itself out in time. Or just pretending that it's not a problem for fear of losing the argument to the divisive political forces gaining pace in many countries. One of the lessons from around the world is that a 'hands-off' approach to social integration simply doesn't work. And without action, the situation will only get worse.

That's why I believe one of the most important tasks now for cities around the world is to take pro-active steps to build stronger and more integrated communities. This means we need to start encouraging and facilitating greater social integration wherever we can – looking to grow social ties and bonds of trust between people of all backgrounds.

I'm not saying that people should be forced to drop their cultures and traditions. We all have layers of identity which are the foundations of who we are and our character, whether it's our faith, nationality or heritage. And we should never let anyone tell us that these can't be compatible.

Promoting social integration is a matter for everyone, for every citizen of our cities. It means ensuring that people of different faiths, ethnicities, sexualities, social backgrounds and generations don't just tolerate one another or live side by side but meet, mix and forge relationships as friends and neighbours as well as citizens.

This is so important because it helps to grow trust and allow communities to flourish. So through creating opportunities for people to come together within communities, we can build kinder and more empathetic cities and ensure that our growing diversity strengthens rather than erodes the social fabric of our neighbourhoods. This is the way to a more productive, healthier, safer and, ultimately, more prosperous city for everyone.

Dawn French
Actor, Comedian, Presenter and Writer
My mum used to say that 'the only way out is through.'

It is so true, and I remember that advice almost daily when I need to find some courage.

Selwyn Jones
Treorchy Male Voice Choir
Family is everything. Cherish every moment you have with each and every one of them. Love and laugh as much as you can for as long as you can.

Joining a choir is like belonging to a new family. Such is the friendship one can find. All members with one aim of enjoying the singing and performing to appreciative audiences. Learning new pieces is a challenge but when accomplished you feel great satisfaction especially when performing at concerts.

Remember, music is the food of love.

Robin Ince
Comedian, Actor and Writer

"The problem is that we judge everyone else from the exterior and ourselves from the interior".

This is what I was told while researching a book on why we become who we become and how we deal with the situation of being "us".

I think we can spend so much of our life painfully manipulating ourselves into the shape we think we should be and ignoring who we really are because we think it doesn't fit with the narrow rules.

For years, I played the part of a performer; sometime in middle age, I managed to defeat the critical voice that would give commentary throughout a show – "You are not doing this like you are meant to if you are a comic – follow the rules – follow the rules."

With that comes impostor syndrome (which is an impostor itself as it is not actually a syndrome).

I am no longer an impostor, I am just me and I have stopped concealing much of myself, not just on stage, but in life. I am much better at expressing love and joy and far keener to do that than share indifference or negativity.

If you take the risk of being open, you often find that this gives permission for others to reveal what they have been hiding too. The greater the disparity between how you project yourself and who you are on the inside, I think the greater the unhappiness and frustration.

I often play David Bowie's "Rock n Roll Suicide" in my head and the effect of the line "Oh no love, you're not alone" is as powerful now as when I first heard it. There are too many people hiding, too many people alone even when they are surrounded by people. Life is too short for people to live in unneeded unhappiness. Opening up can lead to wondrous places.

Sir Philip Pullman
Writer

This is the most important thing I know…

Any statement of the form:

X is [only, just, simply, nothing but, no more than, merely, etc] Y (for example, the famous statement by Francis Crick that, 'You, your joys and your sorrows, your memories and your inhibitions, your sense of identity and free will, are in fact no more than the behaviour of a vast assembly of nerve cells and their associated molecules') …

… is wrong.

Nothing is only itself. Everything – person, object, action, thought, everything that exists – exists in a network of relationships, connections, resemblances, fields, influences, with everything else, from the smallest possible scale to the very largest.

I do know a few other things, but this is by far the most important; and I know it's true, because fifty-two years ago I saw it in a vision on Hammersmith Bridge.

Francis O'Gorman
Writer

When I wrote *Worrying: A Literary and Cultural History* (2015) I didn't realise I had created an open goal.

Last year, when I was diagnosed with a rare and aggressive form of salivary duct cancer, I could hear my own voice saying: "Well, after all that fussing about minor anxieties, now you do have something to worry about."

That was true.

And worrying about this horrible thing, which has invaded my body and is currently held at bay after surgery by radiotherapy, is certainly not a part-time occupation. "Worrying", however, isn't the word for a lot of the experience, which is close not to an irritating back-of-the-mind bother, but, alas, to despair. Being confronted with news of an incurable cancer is terrifying (when it is not for a while merely a nuisance: "I am too busy for this!" "No! I have other things to do next year!"). For sure, this health news seeps everywhere.

Illness has made me spend a lot of time thinking about hard, possibly unwise questions, such as ones about past decisions and the shape of my life. Somewhere in my head I had always, as a worrier, thought about this kind of thing. But not under the same pressure. I ask myself with a new sharpness whether I was right to have made this or that decision years ago: subjects at university, careers, places to live, people to sleep with (to say nothing of people to live with). And I wonder: did I do the right thing? Did I do the best thing?

These questions, grown in urgency, have made me a different person from myself.

Yet one idea, perhaps constructive, has emerged over the past year – and I don't know where it came from – which has changed my sense of the past, and, in turn, future. And that idea has made the future a tiny bit easier to contemplate, to 'live towards'. So if I had a nugget I'd like someone else to know before I am no longer here, this is it.

Looking back over the 55 years of my life, I wish I had questioned my sense – as it seems to me, retrospectively – that I was entitled to things. Worrying might have been an oblique expression of this, I think, but that's an idea I haven't yet understood properly. If I figure it out, I'll try to write something about it.

I can see myself now, as a teenager, at university, as a writer starting out on an academic career, as a mid-career professional pursuing what I wanted and what I thought was good. I can see myself, more personally, rarely questioning that I should have interesting friends, a nice house, good food and wine, holidays abroad, a decent style of comfort, smart clothes. I assumed that I'd always share these happily with a partner.

And now I look back and realise there was – how did I not see this? – a moral miscalculation. An ugly arrogance.

Such expectations can be the source of achievement, I guess. You can't get up in the morning and think: "I'm not worth a good job or a nice house therefore I am going back to bed." Getting up in the morning and assuming that the day is going to be worthwhile, shared with interesting people, and materially comfortable, is a motivator to make sure it is.

But unthinkingly assuming I had a right to such good things, as once I did, isn't the best way to look to the future under the cloudy conditions I now, half-unnerved, inhabit. This is what I have to tell myself during the day. I am not entitled. I can't be aggrieved or angry that I am sick; there is nothing in the order of the world that means I should be happy or well; no fixed fact of nature guarantees me a safe day ahead, the security of knowing that life is coming to me on my terms.

If I try to remember that then I realise that there is more space, more light and air, around me than I had understood. I find that I'm less oppressed, less imprisoned, by the wrongness of things. I don't have a right to be well – and here I am, ill. So that is a condition I must make part of who I am, and live with it, live in it. Setting entitlement aside opens up for me the possibility of making a better accommodation with how I must now be.

Lady Sarra and Sir Chris Hoy MBE
Bliss Ambassador and Olympic Cyclist (11 x World Champion, 6 x Olympic Champion and Olympic Silver Medallist)
In 2014, Chris and I had a baby boy named Callum. He was eleven weeks premature.

Like a baby bird fallen from his nest, he was fragile, vulnerable and a featherweight 2lbs.

He was taken to an intensive care unit and remained in hospital for almost two months before he came home. He is now a wonderfully energetic, loud and hilarious eight year old.

We have learned so much from our son.

Having a premature or sick baby who needs specialist care in hospital can be overwhelming. As parents, at times we felt redundant and helpless. We were consumed by the horror of the separation and isolation from our baby and had to cope with the fear, anxiety and worry every day.

Learning how to be a parent is hard at the best of times, but the difficulty is amplified while negotiating a neo-natal stay. It adds a layer of complexity and stress that can take many weeks, months and even years to recover from.

When faced with the unexpected, it is easy to feel lonely and isolated.

As a listening volunteer at the Samaritans and having spent many years speaking to other families and parents through my work with Bliss, I have learned that while all of our stories differ, it is the feelings that connect us to one another. The feelings are the same.

If you can find the courage to honestly share your pain with someone else, you will find someone who can identify with your feelings. Imagine how it feels to share one of your darkest thoughts out loud, and for someone to say, 'I understand. I felt the same.' No one is so extraordinary that they are alone in feeling the way they do.

There is so much pressure on parents to be perfect, to cope with everything, and to have all of the answers. But we all learn as we go.

So our final piece of advice is simply to keep trying. What would we say to our children? We would encourage them and say, 'Keep going, don't worry about that mistake, give it another go, try again.'

Imagine if we counselled ourselves in the same way.

Dr Amra Bone
Lecturer, Chaplain and Shariah Council Judge
Peace amidst the chaos.

I regularly see many people with mental pain and suffering. Sometimes it can be intense.

As a mother, a wife, a lecturer, a chaplain, a shariah council judge, a reviewer, supporting those who seek help of many types and in many ways my mind can become overwhelmed. Sometimes it seems impossible to manage all the different demands on me. There is so much I need to do, or I must do, as I am the only woman there to do it. We carry so many burdens on our shoulders.

I cherish the Islamic concept of letting go through the five daily prayers, or salah – uncluttering the mind and connecting to the higher force beyond this mundane world, to the ultimate reality. Achieving a moment of consciousness through placing my head on the ground in a physical display of total surrender. A reminder that I don't know everything, reinforcing a sense of humility and acknowledging that I too need help and guidance. Connecting to the higher source to free my mind from the whispers that beset it and threaten to overwhelm it and achieving a palpable sense of peace to provide some respite from the eternal battle.

Sophie Tebbetts
Head of Programmes at FoodCycle
'Just remember you are completely unique, just like everybody else'.

A life well spent is all about the relationships we build and the connections we have around us, and FoodCycle's aim of connecting communities was one of the key motivators for me joining the charity. We believe in the power and many benefits of people, from all backgrounds and walks of life, connecting over delicious food. By offering a safe space to share a meal, barriers are broken down, conversations flow and friendships are formed. Our uniqueness is our commonality. Everyone deserves good food and good conversation.

So don't be afraid to smile at a stranger, say hello or strike up a conversation. You never know who you might meet.

Chris McCausland
Actor and Comedian
It's easy sometimes to look at other people and feel envious of what they have, or who they are, or how they carry themselves.

It's easy to wish that we could swap our own less than perfect life in order to have what they have and walk in their shoes. After all, they have all the luck, they have it nailed, they have their act together.

But the truth is, there is always much more going on behind the curtains of other people's lives than we are permitted to glimpse for ourselves.

Every single person is better off and worse off than every other single person, in countless complex ways that you can't even begin to fathom.

So, just be glad to be you, and grateful you aren't one of these other complicated and flawed humans you sometimes wish you could be.

Enjoy whatever little pieces of perfect you can muster, because you have managed to muster them and they are perfect to you alone. Let all of the trouble in your life make you stronger, because it beats wallowing in the stench of it in the hope that it will magically turn to roses.

Just be glad to be you.

Geoff Dyer
Author

I am so wise! A few years ago I assumed that it wasn't possible to get any wiser but I am constantly amazing myself by coming up with new and profound insights into the human predicament.

Yesterday a friend was bidding for a rug in an online auction even though she didn't love it. 'If you don't love it you don't want it,' I said. It was too late by then. She was in a frenzy of covetousness and said the important thing was that it was the right size for her room so she kept bidding, like a crazed addict, eventually won the auction and became the owner of this rug which I thought looked so dreary I wouldn't have bid a penny for it.

That's an example of what might be called wasted wisdom.

Ten years ago, however, I passed on to a friend my advice on the safe-keeping of spectacles: 'If they're not on your face, they should be in their case.' My friend has never forgotten this and his life massively improved as a result.

That's an example of what I call enduring or 20/20 wisdom. I hope others will follow my teachings.

I keep thinking about that rug my other friend bought.

It really was dreary.

Laura Stamp
Lead Nurse Recipient Coordinator, NHS Blood and Transplant

When I was a child, I had a tendency to worry.

Worries got bigger and bigger in my little head. I told my father that I was worrying about lots of things and he said: "Take each individual worry, and if you can change it, change it tomorrow. If you can't change it, then there's no point in worrying about it."

That really helped me rationalise all my worries, and gave me back some much needed perspective.

I have carried this through my adult life, and apply it whenever needed. More often than not I feel instantly better.

Zara Mohammed
Secretary General of the Muslim Council of Britain
Don't lose your nerve.

I have found in life we have to be bold and confident to keep taking strides forward, to imagine that we can do more – and then when we find ourselves in places we couldn't imagine, to keep going, taking another step, with a warm smile.

I have found that it's exactly at the moment you want to give up and when you doubt yourself that you have to hold your nerve and keep going.

Vijay Luthra
Renal Transplantee, Healthcare and Life Sciences Consultant
Nugget A: Friends told me the fire in my eyes had gone out. Gaunt with an unnatural skin hue and wheezing, along with my eyes pale I looked like I was going to die soon.

Dialysis and then a kidney transplant saved me.

It gave me a second chance. The fire in my eyes was relit. Burning more intensely than ever.

Second chances don't come along very often so I've seized mine.

And that's all any of us can do – take the chance we are offered and strive to do the best we can to make an impact on this world.

Nugget B: We take bananas for granted. Yet for thousands of people in the UK, eating even one banana could be fatal.

The high level of potassium in bananas (and their lovely taste) is why we treasure them. Yet for those with kidney failure, unable to metabolise the potassium, it can lead to a heart attack.

That's why you sometimes see bunches of bananas by kidney transplant recipients' beds. The simplest of pleasures, denied for so long, suddenly becomes possible again.

Never take the simple pleasures for granted, and look after your kidneys. You need them!

Wendy Cope OBE
Poet

I have a notebook where I write quotations I want to remember. Here is a small selection.

> The only end of writing is to enable the readers better to enjoy life or better to endure it.
> SAMUEL JOHNSON

> True ease in writing comes from art, not chance
> As those move easiest who have learned to dance.
> ALEXANDER POPE

> I rhyme
> To see myself, to set the darkness echoing.
> SEAMUS HEANEY

> I give to the world what I feel in my heart and that is the end of it.
> FRANZ SCHUBERT

> Integrity has a power which opportunism can never reach.
> STEFAN COLLINI

> Dare to be true.
> GEORGE HERBERT

Dame Clare Moriarty
Chief Executive of Citizens Advice

Ask yourself what, in six months' time, you'll wish you'd done six months ago? Do it now.

It's very easy to get lost in the day-to-day and lose sight of the bigger picture. This act of checking in with and questioning yourself is a great way to focus on what really matters, whether that's the changes or impact you want to have at work, or something you want to achieve personally.

> **The truth is always complex.**

David Baddiel
Comedian, Television presenter, Screenwriter and Writer

Professor Jason Arday
Professor of Sociology of Education, University of Cambridge and Trustee of the Runnymede Trust

Potential is something we are all born with, converting this into something great requires something even more special... courage, belief and humility.

Understanding the power of grace is important; learning to win and lose with grace is everything. The lessons learned in 'losing' shape how you win with humility.

Success is associated with winning... but adversity and how you deal with not always finishing first on the podium is what builds character.

Love and compassion are essential ingredients to win in life. Always ask yourself: Who did I help along the way? Who did I bring with me? And perhaps most importantly, was I able to positively impact people that I was fortunate enough to meet?

Your potential is boundless and you are great beyond measure. You have all the potential to be whatever you want to be. Your dreams sit in the lap of fate and destiny, but the journey to your destination will be the defining factor in how you realise your potential.

The bigger picture and the positive impact you can make on the world and people around you will always be the most important thing.

Always try to win with humility and grace and always try to lose with humility and grace. May your hopes, dreams and aspirations carry you through all of your days. Always give thanks to the people around you who also cradle your hopes and dreams.

And when the moment takes you, excuse yourself and kiss the sky to the stars and angels always watching over you.

My name is Jason Arday and I believe nothing is insurmountable and everything is possible, with faith, hope, humility and dancing feet.

Sir Mark Elder
Conductor, Director of the Halle Orchestra

Fifty or so years ago, when I started to try and conduct, I was aware of the testing nature of some of the conversations I needed to have with different people.

Sensitive, tricky, delicate they often were, on a whole range of different topics. And all too frequently, they did not go right; I did not manage them well enough.

As the years went by, I gradually learnt to wait, to trust that the right moment to address a problem would present itself, as long as I was open to recognise that right moment. I realised that I needed to keep the issue clear in my mind but not worry about it, just remain receptive. Sometimes months would go by and the opportunity never presented itself. Then suddenly, there it was.

My experience is that, little by little, I became better at finding the right way to express the problem and suggest its solution.

Crucial, of course, is being aware of the feelings of the other person or people concerned.

The nugget might be:

Reflect – wait – be calm, and all's well that ends well.

I remember the time when the word "nugget" felt new and strange.

I was in Los Angeles, rehearsing with some singers. After the session we all went to eat together. One of our number was a wonderful singer but extremely "heavy"! I could not believe my ears as she ordered her main course and an extra serving of chicken nuggets!

What an introduction to the word!

Professor Jagbir Jhutti-Johal OBE
Professor of Sikh Studies, University of Birmingham,
Author and Media Commentator

In a world where we see religious, racial and gender inequality and discrimination, the teachings within our Eternal Guru, the Guru Granth Sahib (Sikh holy scripture), reminds one of our universal fraternity and the need to build a just and equal world in which everyone is respected and valued irrespective of their religion, gender, race or social and economic class.

It highlights that this is achieved when we recognise that all of creation was created by the Divine and is a manifestation of the Divine.

Recognize the Lord's Light within all, and do not consider social class or status; there are no classes or castes in the world hereafter. (Guru Granth Sahib, Guru Nanak: Ang 349)

The Lord Finkelstein OBE
Journalist and Politician

For some people the word "suburb" is synonymous with banality and boredom, a sort of soporific stability that dulls the creative instinct and insulates people from the edgy reality of the metropolis, cocooned and complacent.

But that's not how it seems to me. My mother was in Belsen and my father in Siberia and Pinner is nicer. The reason we fight wars and resist tyrants, combat disease and strike out with new ideas is so that people can enjoy peace and stability, to prosper and live in safety with their families. Yes the heroes of history have often lived strenuous lives, but what would be the point of them if strenuousness was all there ever was?

Patrick Barrie and Matthew Rose
World Tiddlywinks Champions

Everyone is interesting – some may even play in tiddlywinks tournaments.

You can improve with practice and perseverance, even if you don't think you are currently good at tiddlywinks.

Keep a sense of perspective – there are some worse things in life than losing a game of tiddlywinks.

Stay positive – there is always a chance a lucky shot will snatch victory from the jaws of defeat.

Embrace the unexpected – you can't always predict the outcome of your shots.

Take up a hobby – all tiddlywinks and no play is bad for your mental health.

You can still be a good person even if you are bottom of the tiddlywinks world ratings.

Michael Adams
Chess Grandmaster

Your current skill level is less important than the ability to keep on improving.

You can't maximise your potential without being realistic about your strengths and weaknesses, and tailoring your strategy accordingly.

Su Pollard
Actor and Singer

I have always been a believer in self-hugging when one is faced with adversity in any form.

You put both arms around yourself and hug until you are almost breathless, all the while saying to yourself, 'Everything is going to be fine' several times.

When you feel you have hugged yourself enough, release your arms and smile. I find it works every time and you feel renewed. I hope it works for you.

Dr Barney McAweaney
Anaesthetist

It was just another day.

It had all gone according to plan, swimmingly even, until suddenly it all collapsed.

The preparation had been thorough. Meticulous. Protocols followed, textbook, you could say, but I was speechless and so reduced.

In the aftermath, the silence of introspection was quickly overwhelmed by self-reproach, fear, sadness, and a gaping chasm of self-doubt. Tears washed me back to my younger, vulnerable self, devoid of the stoic obligations of adulthood, and I just wanted human contact, a hug.

In that moment, I felt time had simply furnished me with the onerous cloak of adulthood; it had aged me, and I wasn't really ready yet to grow up at age 55 with 35 years in the medical profession.

This was a moment.

As humans do, I wear my armour of belonging, happiness, joviality, professionalism. I work with pride, but arrows do find gaps, and all adults are prone to doubt, sadness, fear, insecurity like any child.

My pursuit of the aforementioned hug ultimately led me back to me. A person I had somehow neglected for some time. Deadlines, duty, obligations and routine can all inadvertently dilute your sense of self and human value. But every day starts with you; make peace with that person as a priority. That peace can shield you from some of life's challenges, and it can foster the joy, delight, and the sense of wonder that you own.

In a world where human communication is practised by fingertips, not lips, it's important to sometimes look inward rather than out to find a reliable friend, and then begin the conversations which the techno-Covid era has robbed us of. We all need those at the minute, and indeed grieve for the lack of them.

Figen Murray OBE
Writer and Public Speaker

My son Martyn was one of twenty-two people murdered in the Manchester Arena terrorist attack on 22nd May 2017. That day my whole world came crashing down on me. I knew instantly that life as it was before would change completely and forever.

At the time I was a busy psychotherapist with my own private practice. Family life was also hectic with five children and four grandchildren and a house to run. Life was frantic at times, but good. Until the day of the attack. Numbness, shock and disbelief took over.

Three days after the attack I saw the face of Martyn's murderer for the first time in the newspapers. I was shocked at his young age. He was twenty-two years old. Over the next couple of weeks, I pondered and reflected a lot on what happened and why. Four weeks after the attack I decided to go on TV to publicly forgive the terrorist.

Despite people calling me deluded, mad or superficial I knew exactly what I was doing. The decision to forgive was important for so many reasons.

Immediately after the attack Islamophobia rose by 300% in Greater Manchester. I felt as the mother of a person killed in this attack, I had the opportunity to break that cycle of hate by publicly forgiving.

But it was more than that.

I had four other children, four grandchildren, a husband, a home to run and I had many other roles I needed to continue to function in. Forgiveness enabled me to continue to do just that. Forgiveness stopped me from being consumed by anger and hate, two burdens that would have been heavy. Two burdens that would have closed my heart to love, kindness, hope and positivity.

Forgiveness is not forgetting or condoning what happened; it is not excusing the murder of my child. It is also not minimising the abyss of my grief nor is it a way of suppressing my anger. There was nothing to suppress as I never felt anger towards the terrorist. The terrorist threw his life away for the real culprit, the ideology he thought was his truth. I was never angry with the young man, the terrorist, the foolish boy who allowed his soul to be hijacked by the devil.

I realised that my forgiveness was never about the terrorist, it was about me needing to protect my heart from being held hostage, it was about me keeping Martyn's death free from contamination of anger and hate. Martyn was kind and he loved people. Had I bought into anger and hate I would have allowed the very essence of him to be negated.

My forgiveness allowed me to walk on a path free of hate, anger, resentment, the need to retaliate and many other negative emotions. Instead, it has allowed me to love more, live more, care more, appreciate more, be more authentic, be more at peace despite my incredibly painful grief.

Forgiveness is what I chose, and it was the best and most important decision I ever made.

Tracy-Ann Oberman
Actor and Playwright

Everyone is frightened and everyone is insecure.

When you can accept that this is the common denominator for all of us, then you can accept that you might know what's best for you.

When you can become your own best friend, your own cheerleader and know what you stand for – then living a life of predominantly joyfulness becomes so much easier.

Katy Sexton MBE
Swimmer (2003 200m Backstroke World Champion)

When times are tough, you are tougher.

It's a statement that I once received in a card when I was struggling with nerves before a competition. It has always stuck with me and I feel covers a lot of situations in life. Definitely my go-to motto!

Steve Backshall MBE
Naturalist, Explorer, Presenter and Writer

My mum taught me 'It is better to give than to receive'.

It sounds obvious but it is true.

If you feel there is something missing in life, perhaps it is not something you need to have but something you need to give.

Altruism is the most rewarding thing in the world. Nothing gives you a greater sense of satisfaction than helping or giving something, particularly if it is something that you really treasure.

Jonny Benjamin MBE
Mental Health Charity Founder, mental health campaigner and Vlogger

When I was diagnosed with schizoaffective disorder, a combination of schizophrenia and depression, I believed I had been handed a life sentence.

I was weeks away from my 21st birthday, and instantly felt there was no future.

I escaped from the psychiatric hospital in North London where I had been admitted and went to a bridge to take my own life.

Whilst on the edge of the bridge, I was approached by a kind, calm, warm young man who spent the next half hour trying to talk me down.

It was an extremely difficult conversation. I was deeply ashamed and embarrassed about my mental illness, as well as my sexuality, which I was hiding due to my Jewish faith.

However, there were five words which the stranger kept repeating that finally made an impact: "You will get better mate."

I thought I was destined to remain seriously ill for the rest of my life, but this stranger appeared genuinely convinced I would overcome my adversity.

Eventually, he managed to persuade me to climb off the edge of the bridge.

It was at this moment that the police intervened. I was taken away to be sectioned.

Over the next few years, I wrestled to come to terms with everything. I was also diagnosed with Irritable Bowel Disease which proved another serious challenge.

Nevertheless, I persevered, and eventually began to see light at the end of the tunnel. I credit therapy, medication and mindfulness, as well as the support of family and friends, for helping me reach this point.

In 2014, when I was feeling particularly strong, I decided to try to track down the stranger on the bridge so I could thank him for his actions years earlier.

Astonishingly, through the power of social media, we were reunited within weeks.

Thankfully, we both got on so famously that we became firm friends, and even began working together. In 2018 we set up youth mental health charity, Beyond, which is still going strong.

I continue to suffer. I've had relapses in my mental and physical health. However, I always stand by the words of former stranger on the bridge, Neil Laybourn, that I will get better.

And if I can overcome adversity, then I am certain that you can do the same.

The Rt Hon. Lord Navnit Dholakia
A Deputy Leader, Liberal Democrats, House of Lords
I believe that the age of criminal responsibility starting from ten years old is too low. The thinking process in our youngsters is still evolving. I continue to promote private members' bills in Parliament to raise this to twelve.

Some may disagree with me, but there are better ways of dealing with youngsters who offend. Childhood is far too precious to gather a criminal record for the rest of your life. Let us hope that Parliament will see sense in raising the age of criminal responsibility which most western European countries have adopted.

Abdulrazak Gurnah
Writer, Nobel Prize Winner in Literature
Respect yourself and others will come to respect you. That is true about all of us, but especially true about women. That is the meaning of honour.

Tejal Amin
Loving Daughter
There is a quotation from Henry Ford dating back to when he was designing his first car: "If I had asked people what they wanted, they would have said faster horses." It's one I use a lot in my workplace, and one that I feel is relevant for kidney care treatment.

We need bold, transformative and blue sky thinking. Dialysis treatment has only marginally changed over the past eighty years. This is not the time for a faster horse. Our goal isn't to halve dialysis time. Our ambition needs to be much, much greater.

We don't even want a car – we want a flying car equivalent.

My message is simple: we need to think big.

Lady Justice Rose
Justice to the UK Supreme Court
"You are not required to complete the task, but neither are you at liberty to abstain from it." This little nugget of wisdom is attributed to Rabbi Tarfon who lived near Jerusalem at the time of the

destruction of the Second Temple in AD70. Many of his sayings are included in the collection known as "Pirkei Avot", the Sayings of the Fathers. For me this saying is helpful on two levels. At its more profound level, it tells me that even though I cannot, as an individual, solve the world's problems, there is still a value in my making what contribution I can. I may not be able to achieve a perfect result but I should not use that as an excuse to stop trying to improve things even if only in a small way. On a more mundane level, it teaches me to make the best use of whatever small pockets of time I have in my busy day. So if I have half an hour or so between meetings, I try to make the best use of that time to make progress on writing a judgment or a speech, even if I cannot hope to complete the whole task in that time.

Matthew Engel
Writer, Journalist and Editor
I can think of nothing more profound than the remark given currency by the late Queen Elizabeth after the death of Prince Philip, "Grief is the price we pay for love".

She actually borrowed it, as one does, from a British psychiatrist and expert in bereavement, Dr Colin Murray Parkes. She could equally have taken the sentiment from Woody Allen from a scene in his film *Love and Death* in which one character explains, "To love is to suffer. To avoid suffering, one must not love. But then one suffers from not loving. Therefore, to love is to suffer. Not to love is to suffer. To suffer is to suffer. To be happy is to love. To be happy, then, is to suffer, but suffering makes one unhappy. Therefore, to be unhappy one must love, or love to suffer, or suffer from too much happiness. I hope you're getting this down."

Benjamin Zephaniah
Writer and Poet
Nugget A: When talking to people who try to justify censorship, dictatorships, or obstruct intellectual inquiry, I like to say: "I would rather have questions that can't be answered than answers that can't be questioned."

Nugget B: I don't know where I got this from, but it helps my meditation. "What is matter? Never mind. What is mind? No matter."

Nugget C: The anarchist in me always reminds me: "The only good system is a sound system."

Nugget D: Education is a great thing, but there are many educated people who have no compassion, no love, or no empathy. Knowledge is not everything. "Knowledge is knowing that a tomato is a fruit. Wisdom is knowing not to put it in a fruit salad."

Nugget D: Money is not everything. "Some people are so poor, all they have is money."

Nugget E: I say to racists who ask me why we came here: "We did not come to Britain. Britain came to us."

Michael Vincent
Charity Trustee

The challenges we face in life are just stuff. None of us can claim the monopoly on suffering. Every one of us is dealing with an issue.

The challenge we all face is how we talk to ourselves about the stuff that happens to us.

What I am referring to is the meaning or interpretation we attach to these external events that show up.

I woke up one morning in 2013 with no hearing.

The next few weeks were traumatic. I realised that while my ears didn't work, I could still listen through my mind, feel with my heart and engage life around me with my intuition.

Reframing our experiences allows us the opportunity to engage our creative abilities that can support us to deal with our challenge.

Reframing my experiences has taught me a lot about how I function as a human being – reframing is a superhero skill worth cultivating.

Simon Pegg
Actor, Comedian and Screenwriter
A key to happiness is to find the thing you love to do and then get paid to do it.

Lucy Campbell
Surfing Champion (7 x National Women's Surfing Champion)
There are times when we need to learn from our mistakes and move forward – but don't be hard on yourself. Only speak to yourself in a way that you would to friends or family. It's easy to fall into the trap of being our own harshest critic.

Josh Widdicombe
Comedian, Presenter and Actor
You will lose a thousand pounds a year to being an idiot. If you can make your peace with that, your life will be far easier.

Dropping your phone and smashing the screen, losing your passport, shrinking a new jumper in the wash – you can beat yourself up for these things, or you can try to see them as part of the annual tax on your own stupidity that nobody can avoid. The second option is the one that won't ruin your week.

Ann Daniels
Polar Explorer and Motivational Speaker
I have learnt many things in my life, but one thing that has served me well is the understanding that it's not what happens to us that necessarily shapes our future, but how we deal with it. We will all face tragedies and setbacks and I've had my share.

Failing in my bid to reach the North Pole solo in 2005 may not have been the most painful experience I've dealt with, but it changed my perception and set me on a path that was far more worthwhile and personally valuable.

After over two years of hard work planning, training and struggling to raise sponsorship, I had left the shores of Russia alone, somewhat afraid, but with the feeling that my destiny was now between me and the mighty Arctic Ocean. After 21 days battling storms, shifting ice, and encounters with polar bears, I put my tent up. I'd completed 175 miles and was confident I'd got through the worst. The days were getting warmer and my sledge lighter as I worked through my food and fuel.

That evening I called my base manager for our regular sitrep. I could tell immediately from his tone that something was dreadfully wrong, but I didn't expect to be told that my expedition was over.

All permits for every expedition were being removed and a Russian MI8 helicopter was on its way to collect me. No amount of positivity was getting me to the North Pole. My hope of becoming the first woman to sledge haul solo to the North Pole from land was over. There was nothing I could do about it.

I boarded the helicopter devastated and angry that someone else had caused my dream to come crashing down. Whilst riding on that helicopter I began to think about it, to really think about what I'd been through. The adventure I'd had, the honour of sharing the icy wilderness with the mighty polar bear and also what was happening around the world. In December 2004 the Sumatra tsunami had destroyed so many homes, families and lives and I began to think about that. That was a real tragedy, not a failed dream to get to the Pole. And could I, in my heart of hearts, blame someone else for me not getting there? How did I know that I would survive the dangerous Arctic for the remainder of the expedition, or that my next encounter with a polar bear wouldn't end in sorrow?

As I thought about these things, I found peace and pleasure at the wonder of spending three weeks in nature alone. Even relief, at the release from the unimaginable hardships I'd been through.

I let go of my desire to go to the North Pole for the world record, and decided if I was going to put myself through those horrors again, it would be for a bigger purpose.

I looked at doing purely scientific expeditions in the future – something that would add value to this world.

Since then I've completed five scientific expeditions and worked with some of the best teams and institutions in the world. I feel truly blessed to have moved into a new arena on the Arctic Ocean.

Something that may never have happened without the sudden and unexpected end to the solo expedition.

I am acutely aware that nothing changed on that helicopter ride back to civilisation, just how I looked at it.

Tim Vine
Comedian, Actor and Writer

"Serve God and be cheerful".

It's carved in stone above the door of Cheam parochial rooms. My dad would always point it out to me when we drove past it when I was a little boy. He loved it. And now I do too.

Adil Ray OBE
Actor, Comedian and Presenter

My tips for a successful career… first, allow yourself to dream big. That's the fun part.

Second, be honest with yourself by recognising you'll have to roll your sleeves up and pick yourself up from trip-ups along the way.

Third, just do it. Don't wait for someone to tell you to. When you're ready, send in that CV, make that call and write that script. The "doing" is the ultimate success and achievement.

Monisha Rajesh
Journalist and Travel Writer

Over the last thirteen years I've travelled more than 80,000 miles by train, winding around the world and back again. In that time I've encountered everyone from Tibetan nuns and Hindu priests to American runaways, French ecologists and Vietnamese farmers. With passengers as young as four sitting beside me or sleeping above my head, I've spent my time chatting with people from all creeds, castes and cultures, learning about their lives by drawing out their stories. And the one thing that I've learnt is to listen more than I talk. It's during my silence that truths are told, worries are conveyed and advice is doled out in full. Even when I'm not on the rails I know that the less I say the more I'll absorb and the richer I will be for it.

Linda Lusardi
Actor and Television Presenter

Always treat others as you would like to be treated yourself.

Live each day as if it could be your last as you never know what the future holds.

Treasure your family and friends, and remember happiness doesn't come from how much money you have.

Sara Wheeler
Travel Author and Biographer

Some years ago, I walked with an Inupiat native Alaskan in the Brooks Range, north of the Arctic Divide. The sun was setting behind limestone needle peaks, and full slopes of ice foreshadowed the Big Freeze of winter.

Samuel, my friend, worked at the Prudhoe Bay oilfields, where we were headed – up the Dalton Highway, the fabled route that shadows the TransAlaska pipeline from Fairbanks to the Arctic Ocean. As we looked at the last rays of alpenglow fading from the tips of the highest mountains, Samuel said, 'Land of my fathers!' Then he laughed ruefully.

Arguments were blazing far south in DC about onshore drilling rights. 'Nobody wanted this land when my ancestors hunted the tundra for caribou', Samuel continued. He liked oil. It paid his salary at Prudhoe Bay. But he revered the land too. The spirit of his ancestors walked there.

We talked that evening in a Deadhorse bar about the compromise playing out in his own life. Again and again, he used the word balance. Two sides to a story, nuance, balance – I learned the importance of looking at both sides from Samuel.

Simon Calder
Travel Journalist and Broadcaster

Checking a bag in for a flight? Good luck.

Three tips for improving your chances of seeing it again, soon or ever.

To maximise the chance your luggage may deign to join you

on your holiday, choose direct flights where you can rather than connecting services. Many of the cases that get lost or delayed are mishandled during transfers.

Assume that every tag will be torn off as your luggage proceeds through the baggage system. Tape your contact details to the inside of your case.

At check in, bid your luggage a fond farewell as it disappears into the darkness. Assume you will never see the baggage again. You almost certainly will, especially if you follow 1 and 2 above, but the presumption that it is disappearing forever will help focus your mind when packing. Don't check in anything that is precious to you.

Professor Mark Wilson
Neurosurgeon

Living creatures survive across generations because of a natural inbuilt drive to pass on genes. As humans, we have transcended this, with a drive to also pass on thoughts, beliefs and dreams, not just to offspring but to other humans. A form of immortality is reached if others are thinking about us or continuing our thoughts even when our own synapses have long since stopped.

The fear of death and the craving to not be forgotten leads to religions, feuds and wars. Such is the nature of consciousness. These are the intricate connections, mostly in our uniquely large frontal lobes, that make us not only human, but who we are individually – our personality and soul.

But these connections change for many reasons, and appreciating this can bring peace in understanding others.

Some things are well known: traumatic brain injury can disrupt suppressing neurons that lead to disinhibition, which in turn can make people more vulnerable (for example through increasing irritability – over 70% of the prison population and 60% of the homeless population have reported a significant head injury).

Dementia obviously alters people, as does chronic alcohol and drug use.

But what about the mild knocks (physical and psychological) we all get through living and even just getting old, losing neurons and becoming more "set in one's ways"?

People change. Personalities harden. This is before we consider the spectrum of mental health which, while labelled as "psychiatric", is actually neurology that we can't image, or do a blood test for, and don't yet fully understand. History will not look on us kindly for this distinction.

If you can't understand someone's reasoning even when you try to look at it from their point of view, maybe there is a reason neither you nor they are aware of.

Is Nigel from accounts actually annoying because he had a mild hypoxic injury no one recognised at birth? You (and he) will never know. And, of course, it could also be your mind that is being unreasonable.

Most people are good. My nugget is to simply find peace, both with those you can understand and those you cannot. Life is too short for anything else.

Iain Mackenzie
Library Assistant, Communities Department, Western Isles Libraries

I love my job. I spend my days driving round beautiful scenery providing a library service to customers on the islands of Lewis and Harris. Even when the weather takes a turn for the worst, which is often during winter, it is still a privilege to be part of a service that does its utmost to serve the community. For a nugget, I would suggest the Dale Wimbrow poem, *The Man in the Glass*.

> When you get what you want in your struggle for self
> And the world makes you king for a day
> Just go to the mirror and look at yourself
> And see what that man has to say.
>
> For it isn't your father, or mother, or wife
> Whose judgment upon you must pass
> The fellow whose verdict counts most in your life
> Is the one staring back from the glass.

He's the fellow to please – never mind all the rest
For he's with you, clear to the end
And you've passed your most difficult, dangerous test
If the man in the glass is your friend.

You may fool the whole world down the pathway of years
And get pats on the back as you pass
But your final reward will be heartache and tears
If you've cheated the man in the glass.

Karen Snell
Kidney Donor

As a mum of three, finding out I was expecting my fourth child was a wonderful surprise for both myself and my husband, and we counted ourselves blessed. Then during my routine scans our world was rocked. It was discovered that our baby at 27 weeks' gestation had a complication which was affecting his kidney function.

We were given the devastating news that the baby would be born with no renal function. However, a glimmer of hope and life was given, when at 28 weeks' gestation my baby boy underwent his very first operation whilst still in the womb.

With the odds stacked against him and the risk of me going into spontaneous labour and losing him, he held on and was born almost full term at 37 weeks.

Although he was born with chronic renal failure the operation had given him a chance of life, and we believe a life he was fighting for.

Over the following months my baby had many hospital stays. He had numerous blood tests, scans, investigations and then we were told that before he could proceed with a kidney transplant, he would need to undergo major bladder reconstructive surgery to safeguard any potential transplanted kidney. For us as a family it felt like a never-ending rollercoaster. Each time I stayed in hospital with the baby my husband was left juggling work, looking after our other children, and managing hospital visits.

At last our baby reached a crucial milestone on the road to his transplant journey. Finding out I was a match meant that I could be his living donor and give him the ultimate gift of life.

Some of our family and friends saw this as a cure for our baby, and believed that he would be living a normal life.

If only this was true.

I believe it is only those people who experience the transplant journey who fully understand, that it is another form of treatment that can ensure a better quality of life.

To donate an organ is the most selfless act of kindness anyone can give another. For the recipient, life is never taken for granted, because no one is promised tomorrow or even the rest of today. My son, now 18 years of age, is an example of living life to the full. He has a better quality of life and has accepted my gift of a kidney as part of his treatment. He still takes numerous medications and attends hospital frequently.

There are no words that can express the overwhelming sense of pride and hope I have for him. He never stops dreaming and believing in himself, and continues to go forward with gratitude in his heart, for the gift of life and opportunities available to him.

Caring for someone with renal failure can be like walking through a storm. At times it feels like a dark, never-ending chapter, until through the storm a rainbow of hope appears. The journey can be difficult, but never stop pushing and believing.

When you become an organ donor, a miracle happens for the recipient every day of their life, because they are given the opportunity to live another day. That is something I know my son truly values, appreciates and is overwhelmingly thankful for.

Rian Snell
Athlete (4 x World Transplant Champion, European Transplant and Dialysis Games Champion and 3 x European Transplant and Dialysis Bronze)

Athletes from forty-five countries took part in over 20 events in the World Transplant Games in Perth, Australia.

There were over 2,500 transplant recipients, donors and donor families all coming together to celebrate the gift of life and demonstrating the importance of staying healthy and active post-transplant.

Team GB&NI was the biggest team in attendance after the host country, Australia, and returned home with 121 gold, 96 silver and 71 bronze medals.

I got a personal best in long jump, taking a silver medal, then a bronze in the 100m and a bronze in the men's 4x100m relay where I ran the last leg to take the baton home for the team.

This was an experience I will cherish forever, and although my mum was unable to go to watch, she was very much with me every step of the way, as it was only through looking after and cherishing her donated kidney that I was blessed with the opportunity.

My nugget is that life is precious. Live it, love it, cherish the gift.

In 2004, while still in my mum's womb, my parents were told that there was a complication and I was going to be born with renal failure.

To provide me with some chance of survival I underwent my first operation while still in my mum's womb at 28 weeks' gestation, which ultimately gave me a chance of life.

Being born with chronic renal failure, I knew no different, and I existed as my kidney function declined. I remember having to be woken up for school, it taking all my effort to get washed and dressed, and not having the appetite to eat meals like my family and friends. Food had no taste. I was fed through a tube, ensuring that my body received the nutrients it needed, although I would frequently become sick from urinary tract infections.

I would join in running and playing with my friends, but not understand why on so many occasions they could keep on going, but I would have to stop and rest and on many occasions fall asleep.

My hospital visits were plentiful, but they gave me the opportunity to create special friendships and bonds with people who I will always hold dear to my heart. It was an uncertain time for me, making friends with people who were just like me, but then sadly making memory boxes and releasing a special balloon along with a prayer for those taken far too soon, and asking my parents when it will be my time to go.

In July 2008, when I was three, I received the precious gift of a living donor kidney from my mum. Although my life was still to be governed by daily routines and schedules of procedures and medications, I felt alive. My taste buds had begun to kick in and I had the energy to witness both a sunrise and sunset in the same day, which was amazing and certainly not to be taken for granted.

Because of my early experiences I was an anxious child and had developed insecurities. That all began to change after I competed in my first British Transplant Games at four years of age. I felt normal. I wasn't the only one with tubes, or who needed medication. I didn't feel any different to anyone else. My parents could talk to other families in a similar position, and they had a deeper, shared understanding of my experiences.

The British Transplant Games introduced me to the sports that I have grown to love so much, and also took my mind off the procedures and the medication, and allowed me the space to be myself and to flourish.

It was initially my family holiday for the first few years, because the games were a fun way for me to spend a few days making new friends. However my flair for athletics began to shine. I began taking a real interest in trying to beat my performance from the previous year. I was not concerned about being beaten by others, but just wanted to be the best that I could be, and this has only grown with time.

An official working at the games encouraged my mum to sign me up to an athletics club. Since then I haven't looked back. I have grown in confidence. I've made so many incredible friendships over the years with people similar to me, people I know I'll be friends with for the rest of my life. I count myself so lucky to have had the kidney transplant. It ignited my passion for sport and has opened doors in abundance for opportunities and experiences.

I represent my club at county and regional level. I compete in the British Transplant Games, raising awareness of the importance of organ donation. I represent Team GB&NI in the World Transplant Games and the European Transplant and Dialysis

Games. I have medalled numerous times, but it's not about that, it's about inspiring others to live a dream, to never give up, and be the best they can be. I wouldn't be the person I am without that opportunity that gave me life and the possibility to raise organ donation and transplantation awareness through competing. Though I've had a lot of difficulties, I see the transplant I got from my mum as a gift of life and I'm determined to live it to the fullest – thankful for the chance of life she gave me, proud of myself for having the strength to continue moving forward through life's difficult journey.

I never regret a day, because the good days give me happiness, the bad days give me experience, the worst days have been my lessons, but it's the best days that give me my memories and make me the person I am today.

Ama Agbeze MBE
England Netball International (1 x Commonwealth Champion and 1 x Commonwealth Bronze)
Smile. A smile can change your day and can have such a significant impact on someone else's too.

Often the physical act of smiling provokes thoughts and memories of things that brought energy, laughter or fondness to induce the chemicals in your body that make you feel good.

A smile is a game changer.

But it can also mask some awful feelings and thoughts. Be mindful with friends and people you know, to look behind the smile and check it is genuine.

Now, don't even get me started on laughter…

Professor Jeremy Hughes
Professor of Experimental Nephrology, University of Edinburgh
There are two nuggets that I do use with patients and students:
1. It is always best to hope for the best but plan for the worst
   (useful for the initial conversation around dialysis).
2. Aim high and see where you land
   (to encourage students to be aspirational).

" Never criticise or complain about something you cannot or will not change. "

Pauline Quirke
Actor

Professor Stephen Westaby
Emeritus Professor of Cardiac Surgery

As a child each birthday, my mother brought me to a sad lady's house to present her with flowers. In time I learned that her baby had died in the cot next to mine. A blue baby who in 1948 received no treatment and was lost before her father could leave the steelworks to see her.

In the backstreets of Scunthorpe my much loved grandfather smoked and worked in smoke. He taught me to draw and paint and noted that I was ambidextrous. We would walk the dog together in the countryside but one day he fell to his knees clutching his chest. I helped him home during that first heart attack but more followed. In those days nothing could be done and soon he descended into the misery that is severe heart failure. Breathless at rest with swollen ankles and belly. Unable to lie flat in bed. One day when I returned from school the doctor's black Austin Healey was parked outside. Peering through the drawn curtains I saw him propped bolt upright in bed with blood-stained froth pouring from his nose and mouth. A humane shot of morphine helped him pass. He was just 60.

Weeks later the BBC broadcast a program called "Your Life in Their Hands". Surgeons in America had developed a cardiopulmonary bypass machine that allowed them to operate on the heart. So at the age of seven I decided to become a heart surgeon. Eventually it became clear that I had Attention Deficit Disorder, one feature of which is the propensity to hyper focus. And for the whole of my professional life I hyper focused on heart surgery.

Two events at medical school profoundly influenced my career.

The first was severe head trauma playing rugby which rendered me unconscious face down in a muddy puddle. I was transferred back to my teaching hospital which recognised that I had distinct personality changes. I had morphed from shy backstreet kid to disinhibited extrovert and for years I lost the ability to sense fear. This was the Phineas Gage phenomenon named after the 18th century railroad engineer who had a tamping iron blown through his frontal lobes. He ended up in prison, but for me the combination of ambidexterity and lack of inhibitions was the perfect start to a career in cardiac surgery.

The second landmark was Christiaan Barnard's heart transplant in 1967. I listened to him speak in London shortly afterwards, and I made the bold statement that "no treatment needing someone else to die first could ever prove mainstream". That turned out to be correct. There were many thousands of heart failure patients and very few donor organs.

In 1981 I was sent to train in the foremost cardiac unit in North America in order "to learn some discipline". I was given a project to determine why the heart-lung machine in itself caused death in vulnerable patients. I identified the fact that the "Post Perfusion Syndrome" was a whole body inflammatory reaction triggered by contact between blood and certain foreign materials in the bypass circuit. When the manufacturers were informed of the particularly damaging chemicals they removed them from the circuit and heart surgery became safer overnight. Thousands of lives were saved before I even began my career in Britain.

That year, Dr Denton Cooley implanted a totally artificial heart in a patient in Houston. The morning I heard of it hyper focus kicked in and I set out to see it. It sounded like a washing machine in the patient's chest and he died within days. My own obsession with artificial hearts didn't.

In 1986 I was taken on to develop a new cardiothoracic centre in Oxford. Through sheer innovation we went from being the smallest to the second largest unit in the UK within 10 years. I started children's heart surgery, then my own mechanical circulatory support program pioneering American devices that their Food and Drug Administration would not sanction without clinical experience. Houston came to Oxford. This resulted in the world's longest artificial heart survivor by several years when I implanted a novel high speed rotary blood pump which rendered the patient pulseless. Everyone said it couldn't work but from extensive laboratory testing I knew it would. These devices now provide equivalent survival rates to a donor heart.

By the time I retired I had performed twelve thousand heart operations, including many in other countries. Then in 2019 came the invitation to present the opening address for the Chinese Association for Cardiothoracic Surgery. The date was 19th December. The location – the huge conference centre on the banks of the Yangtze River in Wuhan.

I lectured to three thousand surgeons on mechanical circulatory support and was approached by a delegation of doctors and hospital administrators who wanted to talk. They asked about the treatment of severe viral lung infection because I had mentioned my previous experience with swine flu. I naturally asked "which virus?" They responded that it did not yet have a name but many patients were already dying. The rest is history.

I kept in touch with my Chinese counterparts and soon discovered that the lecture hall had been transformed into a vast hospital ward. Moreover it was apparent that it wasn't the virus itself that proved fatal. It was the body's own inflammatory response that caused severe autoimmune lung inflammation. Positive pressure ventilation just made things worse. It was a similar phenomenon to the "Post Perfusion Syndrome" I had worked on many years before. It became apparent that the intensive care unit of admission was as great a risk factor as advanced age or serious co-morbidity. Yet when I suggested trying steroids the powers that be just laughed. No one wanted to hear from a retired old buffer and anyone not brought in directly by the government was ignored.

Months later after fifty thousand more deaths in Britain my hypothesis was verified and steroids became the front line treatment.

As the old song says, "that's the way it is."

I believe my whole career was defined by the hyper focus of Attention Deficit Disorder, that head injury and the grim determination to move on from a disadvantaged start. Almost 50 years after watching that first "Your Life in their Hands" program I was asked to participate in a new series. I implanted an American artificial heart for the cameras and I was told it inspired youngsters to join the profession. Sadly the current devices are not affordable in the NHS so I have developed a unique new blood pump – British and best!

So my message is clear. Don't allow background or disability to hold you back. Follow your star and as Winston said, "Never, never, never give in."

Rob Allen
Bereaved father, Patron and Founder of Sands United FC

There's a term, "the strong, silent type". I'm sure we've all used it, but subconsciously we're agreeing that to be strong, you remain silent.

I think that it takes more strength to speak than to remain silent. To invite people to listen to your thoughts, your fears, to open the door to your pain, and ask them to sit with you as you feel.

That is strength. Never be afraid to speak, to express, but most importantly to feel.

Janice Hamilton
Team Leader, Coniston Mountain Rescue

There is no better feeling than helping someone in need. The "thank yous" we receive go such a long way to making all we do worthwhile. However, I wish to thank those casualties, their families and friends, for their "thank yous." They provide a feeling of self worth which many people lack.

This is what helping someone can do, no matter how small or large the helping hand is. It has a two-way effect.

Robert McCrum
Writer and Editor

About thirty years ago I suffered a mid-life medical emergency a brain-attack described as a right hemisphere haemorrhagic infarct which pitched me into intensive care, followed by more than a year of convalescence, an experience I've charted in two volumes of memoir, *My Year Off* and *Every Third Thought*.

As a long-term patient, making a slow recovery, I became the recipient of many nuggets – the wisdom of the wards. When I reflect on these today, my own and other people's top tips can be summarised as follows:

1. Cultivate slowness. You'll never get it if you don't slow down.

2. Live in the moment. Try to be in-the-room, not remote, or online. Life-saving interactions with doctors are the better for being in-person.

3. KBO.

After more than half an adult life spent in the shadow of ill-health, these tips about the mystery of existence boil down to my one fatalistic, but optimistic prediction: things change.

Harry Redknapp
Former Football Manager (1 x FA Cup Champion)
Only older football fans will remember me as an outside-right for West Ham United in the 1960s.

For younger people, an 'outside-right' was what we called wide midfielders in the olden days – back when we still had rationing, London fogs and black-and-white telly.

I signed for the Hammers as a skinny fifteen-year-old in 1962 and as a Poplar boy I couldn't have been prouder.

The manager who took me on was a man named Ron Greenwood, and he turned out to be a huge influence on me and my career. Not just mine, either. He was a mentor for three of my team-mates who helped win the World Cup for England in 1966 – the captain, Bobby Moore; Geoff Hurst, who scored a hat-trick in the final of course; and Martin Peters, who got the other goal. West Ham 4 West Germany 2!

Ron didn't just know about football. He knew about life, and he'd fought for his country in the War, serving with the RAF in France after D-Day. We all looked up to him and respected him.

It was always worth listening when Ron spoke, but sometimes the words didn't come out quite right. Still, you knew what he meant.

I remember once he said: 'Being given chances, and not taking them. That's what life is all about.'

Now, I don't know if that counts as wisdom, but I still remember it years later, and the words have swum into my mind and made me smile and think of Ron every time a chance in life has fallen my way.

I tell my boys and grandkids the same now. When a door

opens up for you, walk through it. You don't know when the next opportunity will come your way.

Joelle Taylor
TS Eliot Prize-winning Writer, Poet and performer
To write a poem is an act of courage; to perform it is a revolution.

Professor Baroness Susan Greenfield CBE
Neuroscientist, Writer, Broadcaster and Member of the House of Lords
Quotation from Rita Levi-Montalcini (1909-2012): "Do not fear difficult moments: the best comes from them."

Claudia Roden CBE
Writer
My father was a happy man, much loved in his huge extended family in Egypt and liked by everybody throughout his life. There were many reasons why he was so loved. One was that he was the only son and last child after nine girls.

One day he told me his mother had given him an important piece of advice: "Sow seeds, do not sow thorns".

I don't know if he followed that advice but he was good natured and well-meaning and that might have helped his relations with people. Personally I feel happy when I sow seeds and unhappy if I inadvertently sow thorns.

Dr Malcolm Q Russell MBE
Emeritus Medical Director, Air Ambulance Charity, Kent, Surrey & Sussex
I have considered with increasing desperation what original life-lesson I can find to espouse. Slightly worryingly, I'm still searching. Every time I think of something I've found useful, I realise it's an idea that I have stolen, or more accurately been gifted, from someone else. But rather than be depressed by my lack of originality, perhaps I should be glad that I'm able to assimilate important lessons from others and deploy them wherever needed – in seriousness or in humour.

As a doctor, workshop tinkerer and country boy, my lessons come from different places. I have no complaints with how they've helped me along the way.

So, here's my rapid-fire collection of stolen nuggets:

Don't think you have to understand or solve everything yourself – surround yourself by people smarter than you and let them find the answers.

Never eat anything bigger than your own head.

Trust the team you lead – give them direction and let them get on with it and you'll be amazed at the solutions they'll find.

There is nothing more permanent than a temporary solution.

It is easier to seek forgiveness than to ask permission.

If you want to see alien creatures and worlds, get a microscope – it will open a portal into a million new universes. Always ask questions.

Make, create or fix one thing, no matter how small, every day – it's good for your soul, and you get things fixed.

"Better" is the enemy of "good enough", yet also, if something is worth doing, it's worth doing properly.

Measure twice, cut once.

If you think you're going to have a medical emergency, don't go upstairs and definitely don't go in the loft.

If hitting it with a hammer doesn't work, you need a different hammer.

The floor is the biggest shelf that you own.

Allow yourself childish delight in the song of a skylark on a spring day or the silvery race of whirligig beetles on a pond. Never lean sideways on top of a ladder.

Train hard, fight easy.

Is the patient getting the care you would want for your family member? If not, try to do something about it.

There is rarely a situation where duct tape, a cable-tie, the right adhesive or WD40 is not the answer.

Jonathan Jenkins
CEO of London's Air Ambulance

They tell you ultra marathon running is all in the head. And they're right. I took them at their word, and rocked up at the Marathon des Sables – the 250km (six marathons in six days) trawl across the Sahara Desert in 2016 unfit, unprepared but optimistic. Despite the 50 degrees, my resolve held for four of six days, only breaking on the "long day" – 85km non stop. I remember vividly when that little voice inside my head said "give up", "what were you thinking", "you can't do this". I remember walking for 8 hours working out my story of heroic failure for when I got home. And when I stopped, I felt absolutely marvellous. For about 15 minutes.

I had the bloodied feet and the story of the IV drip due to dehydration, to tell that story of derring-do. But I knew, in my heart of hearts, I had given up. My body could have gone further, I simply hadn't been determined enough and gave myself a narrative to give up. As far as the folks at home were concerned, I'd been a hero – and should never have expected to finish, and did as well as anyone could. I felt a fraud taking those plaudits, I disrespected the event and my co-competitors. Despite being hugely overweight and unprepared, I could have done it. I failed in the worst way possible – I gave up. I let down those who sponsored me, my family who worried about me out there, and those who had taken it seriously.

So I went back in 2018 to try again. Fitter, yes. More prepared yes. But when I got off that plane in Morocco I simply knew I was going to finish. The feeling of guilt, failure, embarrassment from 2016 was so powerful that I knew when that little voice came to tell me to give up, I would ignore it. I was either going to finish or be carried off the course. The medal at the end was proof that I had it in me to ignore that voice, no matter what my body said. I wasn't proud of beating the course, I was proud I had beaten my own expectations of what I could achieve.

There is no embarrassment in failure when you've given it all, only learning.

But if you let yourself give up cheaply, you will know it, even if no one else does. It will haunt you. So don't be that person.

Don't give up – you're way stronger than you might think.

Leslie Ash
Actor

My mother taught me: "If you're talking you're not listening, and if you're not listening you're not learning."

Kevin Maynard
Station Manager, Tower Lifeboat Station

In my mid-twenties I realised that I spent too much time worrying about what other people thought of me. I had some good friends and I would pretend to be interested in some of the things that they were to "fit in". One day I realised that life was passing me by and I wasn't doing the things that I enjoyed often enough.

I decided to change and I didn't lose any of my friends. To be honest some of them didn't even notice, and it made me a happier, more confident person being myself. So I would say, be the person you want to be rather than the person you think other people want you to be.

Joanne Harris OBE
Writer

I find littering very annoying. It's a minor but also a major thing: a society that litters is one that also has so little respect for the environment and, consequently, other people. If we had clean streets, a lot of other things would be fixed almost effortlessly.

If you want to know what's important to a culture, learn their language.

Dame Katherine Grainger
Chair of UK Sport and Former Rower (6 x World Champion, 1 x Olympic Champion and 4 x Olympic Silver)

I think there's a voice within us and I think that voice talks a lot of sense.

Sometimes it speaks quietly, sometimes it whispers and sometimes it roars. But it is wise and it knows us as well as anyone does. We should listen to it more. It's not always easy to hear amongst the chaos and speed of daily life. We have things to do, places to be, calls to return, messages to write, deadlines to meet, people to be responsible for. And that never changes, there is always a lot to do. But we need to sometimes stop and see how we are spending that busy time and if it's the right thing for us, if we're happy, if it's what we're here for.

I was once told that everyone has an individual contribution to make in this life – and it will be different from others because we are all different in our own way. It doesn't mean we all have to take on huge challenges or ambitions, but something that in our own way makes an impact or makes things better.

When I started off in sport I had a voice inside me that definitely had ambitions and dreams, and I didn't tell people for quite a while. I followed those dreams and I think I knew instinctively what I wanted to try to achieve, but I was shy about it and didn't feel confident enough to shout about it. I've also heard the voice when there is injustice or unfairness. Again it can be easy to think, 'but what difference can I make?' But how many times throughout history have we seen that everyone can make a difference.

We have one life and we should live it.

Just how we live it is about our choices and every now and again it's worth checking in on that voice inside of us in case it's saying something we haven't listened to about ourselves or have ignored for too long.

Trust yourself.

Alistair Petrie
Actor

A simple act of generosity will change lives.

My father died early on in the pandemic aged 84. Actually he was 21. He was a leap year baby, born on 29th February 1936, so he came of age, then age took him away.

He was a fighter pilot in the Royal Air Force and he travelled all over the world flying in full Top Gun mode, pants on fire.

He was very, very good indeed.

He was a skilled aerobatic pilot, a fine flying instructor, a leader. His flying helmet is in my office, a lightning bolt – now scratched and faded – painted on the side.

So far so glamorous.

He was also a working class boy from essentially a single parent family, living in a small flat in Aberdeen. A remarkable youthful talent as a rugby player and a sharp mind meant he got into the grammar school in Aberdeen. Suggestions were made about how he might play rugby for Scotland or be the first of his family to go to university, but he knew exactly what he wanted to do. He wanted to join the RAF, and that would involve a trip 'down South' for the interview.

But that cost, and money was tight.

There was some angst and a proud family were loath to ask for help to get money for the ticket.

We discovered recently that the local church raised the money for the train fare. Now, I don't know how devout or otherwise the family were but I'm guessing it was more a community donation than anything overtly religious. This proud family quietly accepted the donation and off Dad went. The rest, as they say…

That simple act of generosity has reverberated through the generations. I am here because of that act of generosity, as is my sister. As is her family, my family and the generations that will follow us. My father's responsibility of course was to take that act and make it work – so generosity offered can come with responsibility when accepted – but change lives it did and will continue to do so.

When you remember – make a simple, direct act of generosity towards another. It doesn't have to be financial. A kindly gesture will inspire. But remember, it will – it will – change lives.

Professor Chi-chi Nwanoku CBE
Founder, Artistic and Executive Director, Chineke! Orchestra

Sometimes, no matter how hard you try, things just don't work out. Regardless of how much you want something, inevitably there will be roadblocks along the way. The key is to persevere if it doesn't work out for you the first time, and an important part of persevering is having an interest or passion in what you're doing.

It might sound obvious, but you need to love what you do if you are to truly succeed in it. Not only will a passion for your subject, job or challenge help you to persevere when things go wrong, but doing what you love will give you enormous satisfaction in the long run.

You might spend up to twenty years in education, but your working life could last for over forty years. Who wants to spend those forty or so years doing something that's of no interest to them? Follow your passion, do what you love and you're more likely to succeed.

If you go for an interview and don't get the job, who cares? What are you going to do about it? Try again. Go to another interview. Use the experience of the previous failure to give you more energy to succeed the next time. Just because your first choice didn't work out doesn't mean you've lost anything. The only scenario in which you lose anything is the one in which you give up. And that's because failure is a part of life, perhaps the most important part, as you cannot learn if you never fail. And because you learn from failure, you lose a lot less by failing than you might think.

The Irish playwright Samuel Beckett once wrote: "Ever tried. Ever failed. No matter. Try again. Fail again. Fail better."

This means that life is not a single straight line from school and university to retirement. It's a mess of choices; of chances taken and chances lost; of diverging paths and parallel ones, of successes and failures. And the most important thing to remember is that these chances and paths and successes don't all happen at one particular time. They keep happening all the way through your life.

So if something doesn't work out for you now, you can guarantee there'll be another chance further down the road, and often it'll be something you were not expecting.

Tania Gilbert
Conservationist, Marwell Wildlife
I slept badly that first night with half a mind on the scimitar-horned oryx that I had accompanied from the airport in Tozeur, and half a mind dedicated to the scorpion that I had spied tip-toeing across the floor towards my bed as I had snuggled inside my sleeping bag.

I imagined that it had shimmied up to me in the small hours and was now cosily nestled amongst the folds of the blanket that I had draped over my sleeping bag. It wouldn't be the first time. I gave up on sleep just before dawn.

After giving my trousers a good shake and banging my boots against the wall one last time to dislodge any really determined residents, I dressed and emerged from the guard house alongside the entrance to Dghoumes National Park.

Pale light was starting to creep across the salt pan, just enough to see by but not yet strong enough to ward off the early chill of a clear December morning in southern Tunisia. I would like to give the impression that I was heroically dishevelled *à la* Hollywood, but a sleep-deprived conservationist minutes after waking is really not a pretty sight, and I hoped a cup of tea might magically manifest out of thin air. Conservationists run on tea. Well, this conservationist runs on tea. Apparently some drink coffee, but I really wouldn't trust them.

As no tea appeared, I picked my way across the stony ground towards the trucks to check on their inhabitants. We had all arrived the night before and the humans among us had decided that for welfare and safety reasons we would leave the oryx secure in their transport crates until daylight.

Scimitar-horned oryx, magnificent white and reddish-brown antelopes with slender horns that gracefully arc back over their shoulders in a manner that gives them their name, were once abundant on the semi-arid grasslands that surround the Sahara Desert. Human pressures and long-term drought had driven them to extinction in the wild by 2000, but a large global population had been maintained in zoos and private holdings, and reintroductions had begun for the species back in 1985. Tunisia was a pioneer in this work and Marwell Wildlife had been involved from the beginning. This particular project had taken five years of planning and preparation by an international team driven by the Tunisian Forestry Department and supported by a huge number of individuals and organisations.

Having assured myself that the oryx were well, and still hearing the deafening snores of the rest of the team from the other guard room, I crossed to the reception pens to triple-check if the enclosures were ready to receive the oryx donated to this latest reintroduction project by European and North American zoos.

A few minutes later I felt the familiar prickle when you know you are being watched. In turning, I was surprised to find not a park guard, sleepy conservationist or wolf, but the disapproving eyebrows of a tiny burrowing owl huddled inside its feathers on one of the posts trying to catch the first warming glimmers of sunlight.

The moment was broken by the emergence of the rest of the team, each complaining about the dreadful snoring of the others. We spent the rest of the day releasing the oryx into the reception pens, health-checking each one and introducing them to each other. By evening, the oryx were settled into the enclosure that would be their home for the next month, before being released into the larger acclimatisation pen, and then the park itself several months later. Today, we are 15 years and several generations of oryx on, and the park hosts a healthy population of scimitar-horned oryx.

Sometimes I am overwhelmed by the scale of the biodiversity and climate crises, and the social inequality that sits alongside both, and it is all too easy for anxiety to bleed into despair. When this happens, I remember a group of oryx huddled together in an ever-growing patch of sunlight in their enclosure the first morning after their release, and the species-rich restored national park that once housed little more than the low shrubs that had managed to survive overgrazing by goats.

I know that I am privileged to have seen this for myself, and to have been part of the team that reintroduced the oryx, and I know with cast-iron certainty, that all is not lost.

Mike Brearley OBE
Retired English First-class Cricketer
When I was playing for Middlesex, against Warwickshire at Edgbaston in 1974, a ninety year old ex-cricketer and ex-coach was watching. His name was Tiger Smith. I knew of him from my friend Tom Cartwright, who admired him as a coach. I was not in good form, and asked him if he would watch me, and comment afterwards. I scored seventy-four, but it was a pawky affair. After I

got out, I went to see Tiger. He asked me to hold his walking stick as a bat and play a couple of strokes with it. He then said, "Do you think you'll hit the ball harder if you frown?"

This advice stood me in good stead, whenever I could manage to follow his advice.

Professor Liz Lightstone
Professor of Nephrology, Imperial College London.
1. When I was doing my PhD many years ago, I was doing the final step of a very long and complicated experiment and completely ruined it by inadvertently collecting all the samples for analysis (100s of them) on to one filter paper instead of 100s of filter papers. My very sanguine supervisor took one look at my distraught face, took a very deep breath and said "I always think of all the mistakes you can make and advise my students of each of them; and then someone comes along and shows me a whole new mistake I never even thought of – now I know for next time!!" However much we plan, we can always find ways to make new mistakes, but we learn and move on!
2. One of my favourite quotes – "In a world where you can be anything, be kind."
3. And another – "we rise by lifting others."

Amy Denny
Zoologist, Marwell Zoo
At the end of the day we are all animals.

While we may like to pretend otherwise, humans are driven by so many of the same basic needs and desires. But it is how we differ where animals can teach us so much about living better, less complicated lives.

Working daily with non-human primates uniquely bonds us to their simplified but uncannily similar lives. We all want love, affection, food, a safe and familiar environment. Yet often it is the differences between us and them that are so striking.

The primates I spend my days with are purposeful, direct and considered in their actions. They are more perceptive of their environment and the subtle shifts in atmosphere than anyone gives them credit for. They have goals and adapt to survive, even thrive, with a little help from us. Their world is often a lot simpler and more cooperative than many would assume, particularly when compared to our own lives.

This is why zookeepers take offence at the negative connotations of phrases such as "they acted like animals" or "it was like being in a zoo". Zookeepers gain insight into a world of communication and complex social interaction that we encourage you to listen to and learn from.

Whether a tiny tamarin or a giant gorilla, primates are reliant on their troop to thrive. This, I have found, is the ultimate lesson: look after your troop and they will look after you.

Amanda Levete CBE
Architect, Founder of AL_A

We do our best work when we come up against resistance – it is the fuel that makes us think harder, become more creative and develop bolder ideas for our next project.

When we lose an architectural competition, we see it not as a defeat but as an important part of our repertoire which has as much value as our built work.

If you focus on creating a real sense of culture in an office, the work will look after itself.

Emma Bridgewater
Designer and Entrepreneur

I have a simple but perennial piece of great advice.

In the early years of my business – making pottery in a factory in Stoke on Trent – I was dithering over two good candidates for an important job. My father made this pronouncement: 'Of course you must consider both candidates carefully. Check your interview notes. Take up the references – especially the face to face (or even telephone) unwritten ones which are often more candid. But don't waste too much time and energy on the choice. Because the results flow mainly from the follow through: remember that you are not handing over total control, instead you're going to work together.'

Exhaustive research and creating and considering many possibilities – these are time-consuming habits an entrepreneur can't afford.

I have found this useful when I start to go down a research worm-hole. It's better to make a decision, and start acting upon it with focus and energy.

I hope that's useful to someone else – it can get one past a sticky, indecisive moment.

Paul Burston
Writer

People often ask me if there's a secret to being a writer. If there is, I haven't discovered it yet. The only way to write is to sit down and write. Accept that your first draft will be a mess. Everyone's first draft is a mess. But a messy first draft is a start. It's something you can edit and improve on. So try not to worry about it too much. Enjoy the freedom of it. Make mistakes. Have fun. The real work comes later.

Nick Ross CBE
Broadcaster

There's deep wisdom in the old saying beloved of statisticians: "Correlation does not imply causation".

If I have a cold and it goes away after I've taken a pill it wasn't necessarily the pill that cured the cold. Colds get better anyway. Often it's obvious, and hence the old joke about a railway guard challenging someone who was scattering salt out of the train window. "I'm keeping elephants off the line," insisted the passenger. "But there are no elephants in Clapham Junction," said the guard. "I know," responded the man, "effective isn't it!"

And yet the fallacy is persuasive.

Our brains are hardwired to link cause and effect. That's why the Aztecs sacrificed humans to make the Sun rise and thought that dawn was proof that the gods were sated. It's why millions of people believe in supplements and complementary therapies despite the overwhelming evidence that (for the worried well – and even for most worried sick) they are a waste of money. It's why we think long prison sentences deter crime when usually the arrow of causation points the other way: politicians increase the penalties for an offence because voters are worried about the crime.

Correlation might imply causation but mostly doesn't.

Carry this nugget of caution around in your back pocket. As the Romans would have put it, cum hoc ergo propter hoc. Or in plain English, don't be a twit.

Dr Adnan Sharif
Consultant Nephrologist, University of Birmingham
Many years ago on a beach holiday with the family I was trying to tax my brain by reading some books by the German philosopher Friedrich Nietzsche.

It wasn't exactly light reading but something I was wanting to do for some time. There was a lot of puzzled head scratching and pondering when I was reading but especially so at this wonderfully cryptic and mysterious line: "He who fights with monsters might take care lest he thereby become a monster. And if you gaze for long into an abyss, the abyss gazes also into you."

I remember thinking, "What does it mean, what did Nietzsche want it to mean?" It's one of his most famous quotes and has generated a lot of discussion.

As the years have gone by, I've realised that the line can mean whatever you want it to mean. That is the beauty of it. The sentence means different things to different people at different times of your life. Have a look at the sentence and think about what it means to you.

Liam Quinn
Swaledale Mountain Rescue Team
I left the Armed Forces in 2003 after I was blown up by a hand grenade.

The Army set me free into the big wide world which it had protected me from for some years. How was I going to cope? I'd sustained a frontal lobe brain injury and was suffering from PTSD. I was miserable and could not or would not share my problems. I bottled them up.

That was the worst thing I could have done.

I eventually started to share and discuss my accident, and from the first minute I felt the weight of the world lift from my shoulders.

I continued on my path to recovery and a big part of this was life in the great outdoors, especially the mountain environment. I see this as my happy place, time alone, to unwind and forget about the daily grind of life.

I see myself now as a mental health first aid trainer, as well as a Mountain Rescue Volunteer for Swaledale Mountain Rescue Team, a role I am extremely proud of. I love helping others and see this as a great reward.

My advice is to share your problems with others and get outdoors and spend time in nature.

Jamie Windust
Writer, Public Speaker and Model
There is an African proverb: "The child who is not embraced by the village will burn it down to feel its warmth".

I'm trying to remember to provide warmth to others, and be selfless in times when I am in distress.

Acting selfishly or compulsively, trying to hide from my own feelings, keeps me in one place. It doesn't allow me to live life. By providing warmth to myself and subsequently to others, I am able to understand that hiding from one's feelings only isolates them even further. It makes them scarier than they truly are, becoming the monsters under the bed we check for every night.

I am able to be embraced by those around me if I take action to embrace myself. It is a reminder that there's always been a community out there, even if it can be hard to find. Even if it seems like you have to fight through thorns to get to them. It all starts with us acknowledging the power in being warm.

I interpret the proverb as a reminder that people's actions and destructive ways don't always come from an inherent desire to be malicious. Instead, it's the way they and I and we and you fumble around in the dark, causing damage and pain to those around us, only because we are searching for the light that is love. We are searching for warmth because we haven't always received it. We are scrambling without care to find love, and sometimes that causes the opposite to occur. Blindly scrambling because all we want is to be embraced by the village.

Now I make an effort to listen to people. Listening is the way to understand that people often just need a hug, and to be shown some love.

We are all capable of love, and we are all capable of receiving love – even if we don't think we are. In big ways, and small ways, it's those acts of love that will stop the fire from burning this world to the ground.

Rt Rev. John Arnold
Bishop of Salford

I was surprised when asked to become the Bishop of Salford, in September 2014.

I knew immediately that it was going to require a big change in my life. Although born in Yorkshire, my thirty years of priesthood had all been spent in London. I had never been to Manchester. There was a lot to think about and a lot of new responsibilities to consider, new challenges and experiences. I was certainly nervous about the next step.

I knew that at the ceremony of installation, in December 2014, it was usual to distribute a prayer card for everyone to take away, recording the event. On one side were the simple facts of my installation as Bishop, and the date. But what to put on the other side? A quote from Scripture, perhaps?

Time was moving on quickly and something needed to be chosen. One evening, I chanced upon the phrase, "Stay with us, Lord, on our journey", in a prayer book. I found myself repeating it, over and over again. It was exactly what I needed for myself and for the Diocese to which I was moving. It said it all. So much in seven words.

It was based on the sense of the journey through life. It acknowledged my uncertainty about such a big change in my life. It established that my journey was with others. It suggested that, if we were asking that the Lord travel with us, then we would be going in the right direction and at the right speed. It echoed the trust that we must have in that wonderful phrase at the end of the Gospel of St Matthew when Jesus, leaving his disciples for the last time, says, "Remember, I am with you always…" (Mt 28:20).

The cards were distributed and the reaction was beyond imagining. The little prayer began to appear on Diocesan letterheads, on banners in churches, in liturgies, prayers of intercession and even set to music, at least three times. People have written to me to say how much it means to them, particularly when they are facing challenges and problems. It is the perfect companion prayer for every day. I am grateful to the original author, whoever he or she may be!

Alastair Campbell
Writer, Broadcaster and Strategist
Read books, not newspapers; listen to music, not the news!

Karen Darke MBE
Paralympic Cyclist (Olympic Champion and Olympic Silver Medallist), Paratriathlete Adventurer and Author
Ability is a state of mind not body.

Through my own journey, I have discovered the incredible power we have within us to change our thoughts, our emotions and our energy.

We can all learn to be our own alchemist, to transform unwanted emotions or experiences into gold, be creators of our reality and in doing so improve our performance, our wellbeing, and the world around us.

Sir David Hare
Playwright, Screenwriter and Director
In my play about Oscar Wilde, *The Judas Kiss*, Wilde condemns people who think that morality consists of judging others, when in truth it means judging yourself.

So he says: 'I have never come across anyone in whom the moral sense was dominant, who was not heartless, cruel, vindictive, log-stupid and entirely lacking in the smallest sense of humanity. Moral people are simple beasts.'

It's my favourite quotation.

Her Honour Judge Judy Khan KC
Senior Judge at the Central Criminal Court

In a world in which people sometimes have sharp elbows and big egos, we would do well to remember that we don't have to be that way.

We can achieve so much more, individually and collectively, by supporting and encouraging each other.

In this short life, we should try to be kind and to take pleasure in simple things.

As gratifying as our professional achievements may be, when all is said and done we will be remembered by those we care about not for the letters after our names or our job titles, but for our humanity.

Sir Ronald Cohen
Businessman and Political Figure

"Principles have a cost, but they are always a bargain in the end".

Arthur Barzey
UK Headteacher of the Year 2022–2023, Heron Hall Academy, London

Leading a school in an area of high socio-economic deprivation comes with its challenges, but it can be incredibly rewarding to see students transcend these barriers, smash glass ceilings and build bridges to success.

Instilling a PMA (Positive Mental Attitude) in these students and getting them to believe that their postcode doesn't determine their tax code and their history is not their destiny, is a game changer.

I say to students, "Life isn't about waiting for the storm to pass, it's about learning to dance in the rain. Make your sunshine and bring it into school with you." This is a great reminder to them to try and make the best of the moment – *carpe diem*.

> **A day at a time, live and let live.** It's easy to find the dirt in someone, be the one who finds the gold.

Hermione Norris
Actor

As they grow into young adults, I try to get them to understand that Life is the most difficult exam. Many people fail because they try to copy others, not realising that everyone has a different question paper. Always be the best version of yourself.

I always use every opportunity to remind them that in the journey of life, we pass through pleasure and pain, there will be sunshine and rain, there will be loss and gain, but we must learn to smile again and again.

Equally as important, I get my students to understand that not everyone will like to see them succeed and therefore they must understand that when people throw stones at you it is because you are a good tree full of fruits. They see a lot of harvest in you. Don't go down to their level by throwing stones back. Throw them your fruits so the seeds of yourself may inspire them to change their ways.

Humility is the greatest virtue. I remind staff that some of the most written-about leaders were humble servants: Gandhi, Jesus Christ. Staff always need to remember that equality is the destination, equity is the journey – give more to those students who have less, so they can all realise their potential.

Rachel Cox
Renal Nurse, NHS Ayrshire & Arran (and also donated one of her kidneys to a stranger)
1. Time on dialysis should be used to live your life, to spend time with family, make it count.
2. Be kind to yourself. It is easy to become frustrated in the things you can't do, but focus on things you can do, and enjoy them.
3. Looking after yourself physically, mentally and spiritually is important. Self-care is not selfish but essential.

Jonathan Freedland
Journalist, Broadcaster and Writer
I once heard a story about the man who became President of the United States a century ago. His name was Calvin Coolidge and the story may well be apocryphal.

It was said that White House aides would approach Coolidge

with a problem that seemed to demand urgent presidential resolution. They'd set out the issue and wait for his answer. The president would think awhile and then, quite often, he'd offer a two-word reply: "Bowling ball." That, it came to be understood, was his way of saying: "Next." The issue was parked and the Oval Office discussion would move on.

Except Coolidge meant more than that. "Bowling ball" was shorthand for a philosophy of life. Most problems, the president believed, were like the ball launched by a ten-pin bowler: it would seem to be hurtling towards the pins at great pace, even menace, until, at the last moment, it skewed away and into the gutter. As things turned out, you needn't have worried; what had once looked like an incoming missile had, in the end, strayed off course. The right response had been to do nothing.

Coolidge believed his advisors often got exercised about problems that would, in time, take care of themselves. They were hypothetical dangers, or at least distant ones. And so, often the best course of action was no action. Wait and see. We can cross that bridge when – and, more importantly, if – we come to it.

Now, of course that attitude carries a risk: it can lead to complacency about long term perils. But often it helps to ask yourself: is this really something that has to be dealt with right now or might this worry, one that now seems so pressing, pass? Might this ball, apparently rolling right at me, slide off into the gutter? The trick is to know which ball is on target and which one could well slide away. That's not always easy to judge. Still, this is the small nugget of wisdom I offer. Sometimes it pays to look at a problem and mutter quietly to yourself: "Bowling ball."

Cardinal Vincent Nichols
Archbishop of Westminster and President of the Catholic Bishops' Conference of England and Wales.
For us in the Catholic Church, our saints are nuggets of pure gold: they are a source of endless inspiration and encourage us to change ourselves for the better so that we may enjoy eternal life in the world to come.

One such saint is Augustine. He was a theologian and greatly respected in the Catholic Church and beyond for his deep love of God, which powerfully manifested itself in his profound thinking.

If St Augustine was here today he would ask questions like, "How would I feel if Jesus Christ was sitting here in front of me now?" Not, "How I would feel about Him, the Light of the World", but "How I would feel about me in His presence." What a challenge to reflect on how we really are! But also a potent reminder to strive to be the best we can be.

We can meet this challenge confident in the knowledge that God, our loving Father, sent His only Son to die for us as we are now with all our faults and failings. And by so doing He transformed death into life.

How can we know this?

One of Christianity's earliest tormentors was Saul who later became St Paul the Apostle, after his conversion on the road to Damascus. Following his conversion, however, he changed beyond measure and is now renowned for his positive influence on Christianity and, indeed, for his many writings.

In his letter to the Galatians, for example, St Paul assures us that Christ is The One sent by God to redeem us. He makes it plain that we are truly sons and daughters of God for "God has sent the Spirit of his Son into our hearts: the Spirit that cries out 'Abba! Father!'" (Gal 4:4-6).

Another great saint who is important to me is St Francis De Sales. I was ordained a bishop on 24th January, which is his Feast day.

St Francis De Sales was the Bishop of Geneva and is revered for his deep faith and gentleness. His teaching is an endless source of hope in the goodness of the Lord and encourages us to be the best we can be as we journey through this life:

"We shall steer safely through every storm, as long as our heart is right, our intention fervent, our courage steadfast, and our trust fixed firmly on God."

Why should we do this? We can find the answer in the following words taken from the Song of Songs (8: 6-7):

"For love is as strong as Death. The flash of it is a flash of fire, a flame for the Lord himself. Love no flood can quench, no torrents drown."

That quotation is also a summary of the Easter story: by dying and rising again, Jesus, the Son of God, destroyed the power of death over us because of his immense love. Therefore, we are called to a daily transformation of ourselves and must never be complacent: dying to our old selves and being reborn until the time of our own death and rebirth into eternal life, our *Dies Natalis*.

Sophie Hannah
Poet and Novelist
My former mentor Anne Grey once said to me, "We do as much harm to ourselves and to others when we take offence as when we give offence."

At first I didn't understand what she meant or how it could be true. Then, years later, I saw that it was one of the wisest and most ground-breaking sayings that I had ever encountered.

When we take offence, we can become defensive and withdraw, or go on the attack. We think, "I'm going to harm that bad person who harmed me." In doing so, we create, rather than avoid, further harm and acrimony in the world. Whereas whenever we decide not to take offence at someone else's words or behaviour, and to say to ourselves instead something like, "They might not have meant it in a hurtful way, so I could give them the benefit of the doubt and carry on being friendly," we resist the temptation to make ourselves a victim and them an aggressor in our story, and give the friendship or relationship a far better chance of continuing happily.

I have done both in the past: taken offence at someone else's words and acted accordingly, and not taken offence and acted accordingly. There is absolutely no doubt in my mind that the former leads to war and enmity, and the latter leads to happier, healed situations.

Dr Sophie Mitchinson
Lead Clinician, Physician Response Unit, Barts Health NHS Trust and London's Air Ambulance
On the (rather protracted) path to my current role I had many setbacks.

I was unsuccessful in a number of job applications. At one point I didn't even score highly enough to be deemed appointable for a job I desperately wanted. Every single one of these knock-backs felt like a failure. They really hurt. However, looking back with the benefit of some years of maturity, I now know that had I been successful in any one of those applications, it probably would have changed my career path significantly, and I'd likely be in a very different place today.

I now realise those setbacks all happened for a reason. They were bumps in the road, helping me get to where I am today. They made me stronger, fight harder, believe in myself more, and ultimately helped me achieve what I have today. So, embrace the disappointment that comes when you don't succeed at something you want. Pick yourself up, dust yourself down, learn from the experience and make yourself better.

One of the most useful things I have read is that people are often so anxious and stressed because they worry and agonise about things they have no control over. Once I began to let go of the things that were out of my control, I began to be much happier and more relaxed.

So, my advice is to concentrate on what you can change, what you can control, and let go of the things you can't.

Benjamin Zand
Journalist, Documentary Maker and Director
Life is overwhelmingly beautiful, always.

It's easy to get distracted, brought down by the rigmarole of every day. The seriousness of reality, of paying bills, caring for others. But if you can allow yourself some distance, some perspective (by going on a walk, sitting in a park) there is so much to be hopeful about. There's so much opportunity, so many places to see, things to do, people to love.

My work takes me to the darkest corners of the world, interviewing people who have experienced real tragedy, but the one thing that always keeps me feeling positive is the incredible ability humans have to adapt, to accept and to look forward.

So, keep looking forward. See every obstacle as an opportunity for growth, and get excited about all the things you haven't done yet. No matter how old or wise or travelled you are, there will always be entire worlds you're yet to experience, so much fun to be had – and isn't that just incredible?

Alex Carlile, Lord Carlile of Berriew
Barrister, Crossbench member of the House of Lords
On 29th March 1946 Renata, eight years old, awoke on board a ship entering the Pool of London. With her was Frederika, in her early thirties, a cousin by marriage. Awaiting them with feelings of love, anticipation and trepidation was Renata's father, Erwin.

Their last meeting had been on 1st September 1939, when Erwin had been called as a reserve medical officer to his Polish cavalry regiment. At that time Renata had been only 23 months old. Orders on the following day sent the regiment on their horses into Hungary: later he made his way across Europe to the UK, arriving in 1940.

Renata's mother, Tosia, died in Auschwitz. Her four grandparents, uncles and aunts, cousins including Frederika's husband, Frezio, and friends, had all been murdered by the Nazis, some herded out of barbarous death trains straight into gas chambers.

Frederika, an audacious Jewish survivor, had protected Renata throughout the War. Renata was moved from place to place, deception to deception. Much had been beyond the traumatic. She had endured hiding under a table for hours as the Gestapo took away her little cousin, and shot her in the street. She had borne the privations of a children's home where she was fed mouse pie for lack of any other meat.

For Renata, London promised fairy tale excitement and security. She barely knew what a daddy was, yet she idealised the security he would offer even in a strange land. As the ship approached Tower Bridge, she saw it as a fairy tale castle, with her father-Prince awaiting her. As they wept together on meeting, Renata, forced into early maturity by her experiences, said to him: "Hello Tatús. Here we are at last. This is Frederika. I think you know her. She is very nice and I think if you are planning to marry again you ought to marry her."

Frederika had acquired a non-Jewish nom de guerre and by then was working as a secretary in the Polish Embassy in Oslo. She returned there, and love letters followed – on the phlegmatic Erwin's side full of passion, from gregarious Frederika, full of caution for Renata's welfare. Some months later, Frederika defected from Poland and married Erwin in Perth, Scotland. They had one child together. Thus it was that I entered this displaced, and ostensibly totally Jewish family, Renata 10 years older and like a second mother to me.

Forward ten years, Renata was at university, and I becoming more curious. Our father was a contented general practitioner in Lancashire. The marriage, formed out of tragedy, succeeded despite my parents being temperamental opposites. Frederika had become Renata's mother. Indeed, I thought she really was Renata's mother, and did not know there had been another. Our Jewish blood and background was never mentioned

I knew nothing of it. Renata had been made to not reveal anything to me. There was no domestic memorial to Tosia, not even a photograph. My mother had talked her way into a meeting with the Anglican Bishop of Manchester, and the whole family became church attenders. I was baptised into the Church of England, was a choirboy for eleven years, and was confirmed. Another Bishop was a close family friend.

When I was ten and the moment came that I was told that Renata had once had "another mummy", I was amazed even by the little of the story explained to me. It drew me even closer to my beloved sister. Yet even then, nothing was mentioned to me about our true Jewish background. It was years later that it surfaced fully, when I was near to adulthood.

Renata has written and published the story of her years in Poland. Searing and compelling, it reminds us of the importance of the essence of our history. Renata married the perfect Englishman, devoted to her and patient with her sometimes anxious and dark feelings about the past. Now she suffers from what is diagnosed as severe dementia, which he and their daughters bear with huge courage. The last time I saw her in her nursing home I only penetrated the confusion in her brain when she joined me in the songs she sang to me when I was little, and read her favourite poem, TS Eliot's *Macavity the Mystery Cat*, which she had taught me as a boy.

I doubt her diagnosis, at least in part. I believe that the unspeakable cruelty and persecution she suffered, the knowledge of her mother having been tortured and murdered, have at least exacerbated her condition and advanced her symptoms.

Over the years we have talked about our suppressed Judaism. We believe our parents made their decisions through fear of recurrent persecution. My mother always travelled with luggage sufficient to enable her to face another episode of living by her wits. We don't blame them for what they did. As a family we have re-discovered, even created, a family record of Tosia's own heroism and suffering. I regret missing being brought up as a Jew, and having so little knowledge of Judaism despite the support of good Jewish friends. It is a serious lacuna in my own life story.

I have commenced a role as Chair of the Woolf Institute's Commission on the Integration of Refugees. Perhaps our parents' and Renata's and my experiences will find some passage there. (Draft of an article for the Jewish Chronicle, November 2022)

Salley Vickers
Novelist

Many years ago I worked for the great theoretical physicist and proponent of the Many Worlds theory, John Archibald Wheeler. He was a man of immense seriousness and depth but also humour and kindness.

He employed me at a time in my life when I had parted from my husband and was alone with two small children in Texas. Among his many pithy maxims was, "We must learn to make the mistakes as fast as possible".

He was referring to science and progress in science but I adopted this as one of my guiding life principles and found it valuable when I went on to train and then to work as a psychoanalyst.

People often think or say, "If only I hadn't ..." citing some mistake they feel they have made which has blighted their life. In fact, mistakes are necessary if we are to learn. Evolution is a series of mistakes which become adaptive.

I would say, speaking now as a novelist, they are essential in the creative sphere. So, whenever I make a mistake, once I have got over the initial feelings of regret, disappointment, self-reproach et cetera, I try to remember that the mistake was almost certainly part of a necessary process of growth or improvement.

Zoe Newnham
Animal Keeper, Marwell Zoo's Rhino Team
Being a zookeeper, working with and forming a close relationship with the animals I work with has made me appreciate life, and especially nature, and how rewarding they can be. Even after a tough day, going to see my favourite species will always put a smile on my face.

They have taught me compassion, patience, resilience, strength and the importance of responsibility, and are the cause of both some of the happiest and saddest days of my life.

They go through some of the same life events we do within their herds or family and social groups: birth, death, illness, change, and as keepers we are right there alongside them. It's amazing how you can form such a close bond with a living being that you do not share a language with.

They have taught me how fragile life and nature can be, and the importance of enjoying every day as much as you can, especially the small things (such as your animals not making as much mess as they usually do for you to clean up!) and how important it is to protect nature for future generations.

David Bailey
Wildlife Photographer
Immerse yourself in nature and everything else is immaterial.

My perfect day is to rise from my slumbers well before the crowing of the cockerel. Drive to the rolling Dorset downlands and walk. Laying out my roll mat with camera gear beside me I relax and doze.

Looking at the stars, I listen to owls calling and other noises of the night while waiting for a glimmer of light from the approaching dawn. Night creeps into day and the world around me takes on a different busy meaning. Hares abound and sometimes visit me, investigating my prone body. Deer bark. Overseeing the world is the cheerful skylark. No matter the time of year it sings its merry song while performing an aerial dance which uplifts my heart.

Nothing, but nothing, else is important when surrounded by nature.

Sarah Hall
Patron of the Humanists UK
For years I've had a little postcard that I've stuck on the walls of each of the houses I've lived in (there have been many).

It's a reproduction of a painting of the northern lights by the Canadian artist AY Jackson. Luminous green, above dark nocturnal mountains. I love what's happening in the painting.

Carl Sagan proposes that the universe is neither benign nor hostile, merely indifferent. True. But humans are part of this universe and are we really indifferent? We seem both malign and benign, and if we assert our indifference how shall we live together?

I'm a rural kid from the Lake District, who always finds solace in nature. Not meaning in nature, or God in nature – I'm also a patron of the Humanists – but solace, a sense of presence and belonging and even peace. I believe in aspiration and striving towards a benign existence, which must accord with our environment as well as fellow humans. My northern lights postcard always reminds me of this concept – even in the darkness, even though the aurora is energised particles from a violent Sun event, brilliance and beauty can occur in our human realm.

Tom Conti
Actor
From my father, a piece of advice that should be given to all boys. In his thick Italian accent, "Don't try to kissin' a girl if she not want you to kissin' her."

Also from him, "Never puttin' cream in carbonara."

From my mother, on my telling her that I was forgoing further education in order to be an actor, "Just remember, everyone needs a plumber."

Also, "You have to learn to keep your mouth shut." I never did.

From Maxine Libson, my friend and PA of many years, in exasperation with me, "If you don't put it back where it's supposed to be, it won't be there when you need it again."

On trying to explain to my daughter, Nina, the purpose of algebra in reducing huge calculations to a manageable formula, "Oh, you mean 'To make a long story short.'" Had my maths master told me that I'd have been better at it.

Years ago, I read wise words from a traffic cop, "When overtaking on a highway, keep an eye on the front wheel of the vehicle you're passing. The first sign that he might be moving out in your direction will be his wheel approaching the white line. Just watching the body of the vehicle isn't as noticeable."

One from me, "When there's a problem with your flight, it's not the fault of the girl on the desk."

Another from me for all actors, "When you or someone else is delivering a laugh line, for God's sake keep still."

Ashley Hickson-Lovence
Writer and Lecturer in Creative Writing

My favourite poet, the late Frank O'Hara, in offering advice about his craft in his 1959 essay, *Personism: A Manifesto*, wrote: "You just go on your nerve".

I have carried these words with me since I first stumbled upon them at school.

When I became the first in my family to go to university, I went on my nerve. When I qualified as a referee as a teenager, the most loathed position on the football pitch, I went on my nerve. When I first sent my books to a literary agent to read, I went on my nerve. When I applied to do a PhD in the hope of becoming a doctor of creative writing, I went on my nerve.

I try to live every day following my gut, rolling the dice, trying my luck, essentially, as O'Hara suggests, going on my nerve.

No matter your background or your so-called credentials on paper or how you or your people may be viewed by some sections of society, always remember, that who you are and where you've come from really matter.

The world is not an easy place sometimes, especially if you're from an already marginalised community, but whatever you want to achieve in life, aim sky high, work hard, be kind to others, go on your nerve and believe.

Vicky McClure MBE
Actor

Play music every day. Look after people. Be on time. Buy less and give more.

Whatever makes you laugh and keeps your heart happy – do that always.

Michael Frayn
Playwright and Writer

Rule One for a healthy old age: always hold on to the banister when you're going downstairs. This to a friend of ours from a distinguished medical man of his acquaintance. To which I might add: "Not a bad idea to hold on to it when you're going upstairs, too."

J
Member of Drug Addicts Anonymous UK

People in Drug Addicts Anonymous come from all walks of life, and come together to recover.

We've all known pain – while we might have blamed our addiction on it before, with time we come to realise the beauty in suffering as it allows us to connect with and help people around us.

Like many others, I also suffer from chronic kidney disease (CKD). On days with high fatigue or other triggers, it's easy to lose yourself in everything that could be better.

When I first came to DAA over three years ago, I felt broken and lost due to my addiction. It is understandable to spend time obsessing over the life we feel we are due, but it kept me stuck. I was yearning for an acceptance and love from external substances, which I was only able to receive from within.

Working through the twelve steps of DAA, I gradually came to let go of the past and lower my defences – to really sit and feel emotions, instead of running away from them. I was then able to see everything I had to be grateful for, and everything I was able to pursue in life. What DAA gave me was a perspective shift without minimising my current circumstances.

Doing the work takes patience, but most importantly compassion for yourself. You cannot force yourself to be ready for change, but when you are, help is there for you if you are brave enough to ask.

After a lifetime of running, I have finally found home within myself.

Juliet Stevenson CBE
Actor

So many user-friendly bits of wisdom have been handed to me by older and smarter people throughout my life. From wonderful actors who helped me deal with the more brutal aspects of our profession, or to hone my craft. From an array of wonderful mothers once I had children – great tips for parenting, and guides to getting through those small domestic challenges. From many others – helping me to deal with the bigger picture.

Many of these nuggets have become my mantras, that help me when life gets confusing, tough, bewildering, mean, hectic, frightening or too much.

To pick one, I would say as I watch the spreading global contagion of cruelty and hatred generated by social media and online bullying; and as we see the powerful increasingly pursue their tunnel-visioned ends with ever diminishing returns to the powerless, the motto, "Do as you would be done by" seems the most appropriate and needed. Or to put it into more ordinary speech, "Treat others as you would like to be treated yourself."

If we all adopted that and put it into practice, the world would be transformed.

And as we observe the terrifying impact of global warming across the continents, from raging forest fires destroying homes and livelihoods, to melting glaciers, parched pastureland and much else; and to see governments fail so drastically to take the appropriate measures, it is easy to feel overwhelmed with pessimism and to give up. But one of my great teenage heroines, Dora Russell, wrote, "Despair is a luxury we cannot afford," and I have clung to that mantra all my life.

So often it has simply and effectively lifted me out of bleak places and galvanised me back on to the front foot.

There is always something we can do. And to be proactive is always better than to be reactive.

Sir Richard J Evans
Historian and Author

Never write for money – what you produce won't be good.

Always follow your nose, research and write about what really interests you, and follow up your leads to the end. You're bound to turn up something interesting if you're persistent enough in your research.

Professor Anil Seth
Professor of Cognitive and Computational Neuroscience, University of Sussex

How things seem is not (necessarily) how they are.

The novelist Anaïs Nin wrote: "We do not see things as they are, we see them as we are".

Modern neuroscience has borne her out.

According to one influential view that I sign up to, even though it seems as though the world pours itself directly into our minds, our experiences of the world around us, and of being a self within this world, are active constructions. They are inside-out, brain-based "best guesses" that are tied to the world, and the body, in ways that have been shaped by evolution to be useful, not to be accurate.

I've found this perspective about the nature of experience surprisingly helpful in life.

Sometimes it's too easy to get into 'perceptual habits' where we experience the world, and the self, in negative ways. We enter a vicious cycle of perceiving things to be going badly, believing them to be going badly, perceiving them even more negatively, and so on into ever gloomier depths. Simply stepping back and recognising that how things seem is not (necessarily) how they are, but an interpretation of how they are, can help break the cycle, depriving it of its self-sustaining energy.

In the space we find between how things seem and how things are lies an opportunity to practise new ways of perceiving, believing and feeling about the way the world is and, more importantly, about the way we are.

Tracy Foster
Chief Guide, Girlguiding
I never thought I would apply to be Chief Guide. But the encouragement and support of others ultimately helped me think, "Why not me? I could make that difference and take up that challenge."

I find asking, "Why not me?" is a great way to flip self-doubt on its head. And that's what Girlguiding is all about – we help all girls know they can do anything.

Michael Ball OBE
Singer, Actor and Presenter
"This too shall pass" is the greatest piece of wisdom we can ever learn.

Nothing, be it good, bad or indifferent, is permanent.

Living the moment – confident in the knowledge that situations and circumstances will always change – should be embraced.

Sir Trevor Phillips OBE
Writer and Broadcaster
Guyana, where my family comes from, was the original inspiration for Walter Raleigh's Eldorado.

We mine gold, often in the form of nuggets – it's one of the things you are given as a child and you keep as a ring, or earrings or a tiepin perhaps. So maybe think of the following as my five gold Nuggets.

First: "Better to light a candle than curse the darkness".

Attributed to the Reverend William Watkinson Lonsdale. While we need to be aware of what is wrong with our circumstances, the best reaction is to do something, however small, rather than simply complain about the problem.

Second: "Every rope got two ends".

Guyanese proverb. There are always (at least) two sides to every argument and we need to hear both before deciding which way to pull.

Third: "If they get you thinking about the wrong question, they don't need to worry about the answer".

Thomas Pynchon, *Gravity's Rainbow*. Good advice for people in politics and media – but even children know how to distract their parents by making the family focus on everything but getting the homework done.

And two from wise women in my family...

"Just because the Devil whistles a tune doesn't make it a bad melody".

From my grandmother, who knew that we can find wisdom even in the most unlikely places.

"You can't draw the map until you've made the journey".

Despite GPS, my younger daughter points out that someone has to make the path for others to follow.

Jules Chappell OBE
Diplomat and Britain's youngest ever Ambassador
(to Guatemala, El Salvador and Honduras)

A fellow diplomat, Charles Crawford, told me, "Focus not on what you're saying, but on what is being heard."

It's a simple reframing but has become a mantra for me. It reminds me that it's so easy to get caught up with our own egos; to fret about what we said in the speech or the important email we sent; to jump in with the things we needed to say right then and there.

In reality, the question is really, "What did others actually hear? What message did they take away? How did it make them feel and what is it that they will remember?"

Thinking about communication this way can change not only what we say but also when and how we choose to say it. Context becomes everything.

Peter Barker
Royal National Lifeboat Institution Crewmember

After 55 years (and counting) as both a volunteer and fulltime RNLI lifeboat crewmember I am sometimes asked, "What was your worst rescue?" I prefer to reflect on the most memorable, of which there are many and not always involving bad weather.

One of my most memorable calls was in August 1999 when along with our colleagues from Ramsgate and Dover lifeboat stations we were called out following a collision between a cruise ship and container vessel.

The cruise ship had 2,400 passengers and while its bow was heavily damaged, fortunately no-one was injured and it was able to limp into Dover.

The container ship came off second best and a fierce fire broke out among containers on deck.

Our role was to provide safety cover as salvage teams from the Netherlands and the UK were airlifted to the ship and tugs fought the blaze with their fire monitors.

The cargo including hazardous materials with the possibility the ship would have to be abandoned if the fire could not be contained.

We also recovered a lifeboat that had fallen from the cruise ship, and towed it to Ramsgate where the lifeboats took turns to refuel and carry out crew changes.

Once the salvors reported the fire under control we were all released and returned to our respective stations.

The fire was extinguished five days later. The call lasted 31 hours for the Margate lifeboat, from launch to recovery – at the time the longest continuous service call since the lifeboat assisted in the evacuation of Dunkirk in 1940. I was one of three crew members who remained on the lifeboat throughout what was a memorable service call with potentially catastrophic consequences.

When the pagers go off, especially as coxswain, your thoughts turn immediately to what the call-out is for.

Aspects include weather conditions and forecast; state of the tide; crew availability including those with specialist skills. It could be a swimmer in difficulties immediately in front of the lifeboat station, or at the other extreme, like the collision between a cruise ship and laden container vessel 15 miles offshore, leading to a fire and a 31-hour call.

You have to be ready for everything. At sea and in life.

Marjorie Wallace CBE
Journalist, Writer and Broadcaster.
Founder and Chief Executive of Mental Health Charity SANE.
As a young child growing up in Africa, I would spend many adventurous weekends on safari with my father, a civil engineer who was mapping the railway lines, and my pianist mother.

"If you meet a lion", she would warn, "don't move. Just stare him in the eyes. If you run away, lions can smell your fear." Whether her advice was biologically or practically wise I am not sure, but her message remained imprinted on me all my life. Face up to your fears; don't ever run away.

I am not talking just about the myriad real threats that we all experience in our often hostile and difficult world. Fear, as we know, is an essential emotion protecting us from danger. I am writing about our own deep-down pernicious thoughts, that kernel of doom and dread inside us which has no shape and no name, but which can overwhelm, leaving us feeling paralysed, panicky and profoundly alone.

This is the fear of the unknown, the sense of loss of identity and the inevitability of death.

But fear – like anxiety, depression and other emotions which elude our rational scrutiny – is an essential part of the fabric of being human.

Apart from alerting us to threats to our survival, it can drive us to meet our deadlines and help achieve important goals.

When I am in the grip of fear, I have found courage by reading stories about people who have pitted their minds and bodies against the elements, spent years in solitary confinement or endured other physical and emotional trauma. Many of the great writers have struggled with these disabling feelings.

Leo Tolstoy graphically describes his own suicidal state: "Every day of life, every step in it, brought me nearer to the edge of a precipice, whence I saw clearly the final ruin before me. I shut my eyes so as not to see the suffering that alone awaited me, the death of all of me, even to annihilation."

It is comforting to remember that despite these terrors, Tolstoy lived a successful life until the age of eighty-two.

Recently when I was in hospital seriously ill with pneumonia, I muttered to myself, "If I die, is this all there is? Has fear kidnapped me by stealth?" Again, I recalled my mother's words about the lion, "Don't run away, don't surrender, look fear in the eyes." Extraordinarily, the haze from my vision cleared, my cough abated and I felt able to face whatever future lay ahead again.

So what can we do to conquer our destructive moods? What can we do to survive those dawn duels when one part of our mind battles with the other?

Fear loves a fight. What it does not like is to meet with quiet strength and gentle understanding.

We need to muster our inner resources, face up to our own failures and learn to forgive our frailties and those of others.

I hope that when you next wake up in the morning your room may feel more empty but you may also find that the hidden dark assassin which has stalked your days and haunted your nights will have disappeared.

Fear itself will have fled, leaving only a small shadow on the white sheets of your bed.

Sheila Coates MBE
Director, SERICC (South Essex Rape and Incest Crisis Centre)
"Never doubt that a small group of committed citizens can change the world. Indeed, it is the only thing that ever has." – Margaret Mead, anthropologist, recipient of the Planetary Citizen of the Year award 1978.

In deciding how to approach the question of a meaningful golden nugget, the question arose, "Is this nugget about me personally or my activist work?" It soon became clear that my activist work is me.

There I was, aged twenty-five in 1981, influenced by what some now refer to as the generation of change. Nationally thirteen thousand women in 1979 had reported an incident of assault and rape, the sexual assault of women and girls was under-reported, socially and politically it was below the radar. I was aware of a diverse group of women who were united by the same aim, to end male violence against women. We wanted to fix the systemic social and political practices that were evidently broken and retraumatising the victims of male sexual violence.

In 1981, as a small local group of five determined and committed activist women asked the question, "do we need a local support group for women who have experienced sexual violence?", the answer of course was "yes".

The next question was so much harder to answer: "How do we do it?"

With the support of other committed women who had already set up a volunteer-led service, by 1983 we had registered as a charity and by 1984 we had opened a support service providing a telephone helpline and one to one meetings giving women victims a space to talk.

From the outset we had begun to uncover the hidden number of victims and their individual experiences. The uncovered need included: child sexual abuse within the family; forced marriage; sexual domestic violence; the profile of perpetrators; the bad practice within the police; the criminal justice system as a whole; social services; mental health services et cetera. This uncovering, solely enabled by the brave women who spoke to us, served to ignite a stronger commitment in us to make change.

At this point, the concept of counselling did not exist in the UK. That was to come later with the arrival of the USA counselling industry. From what was a volunteer-led service offering women an independent non-judgemental space to talk with other women we moved into the counselling qualifications world. To this day, we have managed to retain our original ethos, to provide a range of appropriate and effective services to support adult and child victims and survivors of all forms of sexual violence and abuse in their recovery from trauma and to enable them to have a voice.

We had begun the often difficult and often heart-warming journey of developing our services.

In 2020 we merged with two other sister services to continue to raise awareness and promote greater public understanding of the nature, context and impact of sexual violence and child sexual abuse. From April 2021 to March 2023, our local services provided 33,890 one to one counselling sessions.

It's touching to remember the excitement when our first fundraising jumble sale raised £64.75. The realisation had not yet sunk in that the societal and political failures to adequately acknowledge the needs of victims and survivors of sexual violence and abuse and the ever-intensifying need for funding would become two of the most tedious, exasperating and wearisome elements of our work. This remains so to this present day.

I am now sixty-eight, after forty-two years the work continues and there have been many successes along the way. As committed citizens who wanted change, we are a living, breathing example of Margaret Mead's message.

"Organisations are like living beings. We often think of organisations as created to deliver outputs. However, organisations are not just functional – they are physical, emotional and spiritual. They have souls, and it is each organisation's soul song that keeps its rhythm going, energising and inspiring growth".
(*Making Change Happen: Power*, Valerie Miller, Lisa VeneKlasen, Molly Reilly and Cindy Clark, 2006)

> "I don't feel very wise but I'll borrow my dad's last words: 'Love each other. That's the only thing that matters in the end.'"

Christie Watson
Nurse and Author

Matthew Parris
Writer and Broadcaster

I offer this nugget as a piece of wisdom that my father offered me but which I'm afraid I have consistently failed to harken to, all my life. But that doesn't make it any less true. It is this: "Never miss an opportunity to say nothing".

David Tovey
Artist, Educationalist and Activist

On Easter Sunday 2011 I had a stroke which was the catalyst for my life falling apart.

Within six months I was diagnosed with cancer neurosyphilis and admitted to hospital.

During treatment I had a cardiac arrest which affected my mental health. In one week I tried to take five overdoses, attempting to end my life.

My doctor phoned to say there was a problem with my bloods. I was diagnosed HIV positive.

Then life plodded along for a while. I went to university and tried to change my career to give myself a new outlook on life.

I was still troubled. On June 20th 2013 I took an overdose in a park in central London.

I was lucky as a lifesaver from the nearby leisure centre resuscitated me, called an ambulance and got me into hospital.

That wasn't the end of it. When I left hospital I came back to my flat to find that the locks had been changed and I'd been made homeless.

I was broken, devastated, lost and didn't know what to do. But I was a soldier. I'd spent six years in the forces, so I had this mentality of, "I've got myself into this, I can get myself out." So I moved into my car – a Peugeot 206 – which for a six feet four inches guy is not the best. This became my home for the next six months.

I've never really spoken a lot about my time homeless because it was really awful. I wouldn't wish homelessness on my worst enemy. It destroys your soul. It takes away your choice. It takes away your friends. It takes away your family. As it went on it took away my mind. It broke me. It stole every single little bit of my soul.

I felt the shame and the stigma that is thrown at you daily, and the abuse and the hate that you receive from the public for being in a situation that you never chose.

I got to the stage where I couldn't carry on. I hadn't eaten for three days. We had a major storm and a tree came down and hit my car. I had about 50 parking tickets on my windscreen. I had nowhere to turn. No-one to ask for help. I went into the council office and they threw me out. My HIV had got out of control to the extent that if it was left I would've been dead. My body was falling apart, with blisters so bad on my feet that I couldn't walk.

I made the final decision to end my life because I couldn't see myself waking up the following day.

To be honest I didn't want to.

I went into a locked park, Isledon Gardens in Islington, and sat on a bench. I was crying and rocking. I didn't know what to do. I pulled a syringe from my pocket and two grams of crystal meth and started to inject.

Suddenly a man said, "What are you doing?"

I couldn't answer. I just cried, then sat with him for over two hours, telling him everything. He gave me £10 and got me into a cold weather shelter for the following day, got me back to my car and got me some food.

This is a great man. Not only did he save my life, he gave me my life back. He listened. He cared. His name is Gavin Lane, he's a park enforcement officer in Islington, and he is the most amazing individual I've ever met.

And this is where it gets to my nugget of wisdom...

Everyone tells you that one person can't change the world but I disagree. Gavin is one person, and he changed my world. He gave me that choice to get back on my feet. Hopefully I've done the same, and since that day I've gone on to do so many things, from sitting on government panels, to helping other people who have been in my situation get back on their feet, to get their artwork seen.

I founded a homeless arts festival that has shown artworks from all over the world. I've had artworks exhibited all around the world and have won UK and international art competitions. I've met presidents and prime ministers to talk about homelessness, and how arts has the ability to give people back their souls and provide a pathway to housing. And now I'm co-director of an international charity in the arts and homelessness, working with over 550 organisations worldwide. Our exhibitions show the world that just because we've been homeless, we aren't useless.

Hopefully my work helps my community thrive not just survive, because I can't grow as a person unless my community grows with me.

So when they say one person can't change the world, disagree with them. You can be that person who changes the world for someone, because a twenty second intervention changed my world forever. It only took one great person to change my world, and if he hadn't I wouldn't be here to give you this nugget of wisdom today.

Emilie Vanpoperinghe
Co-Founder and CEO, Oddbox

When I need to make a hard decision, I ask myself, "What's the worst that could happen?" and probe further into the worst-case scenario.

Making a big change is hard, and thinking about the worst can help.

When deciding to be full-time with Oddbox, I asked myself that question and came to the conclusion that in the worst case scenario, I would have to find another job and it actually didn't feel so scary anymore.

Dame Jenni Murray
Broadcaster and Journalist

My mother insisted I should learn to speak well – no Yorkshire accent, though I was born and raised in Barnsley.

She sent me at the age of five to an elocution teacher, Miss Florence de vere Firth, who preferred to call her lessons speech and drama. I went to her every Friday night until I was 18. I performed at local music festivals and took exams at the Guildhall School of Music and Drama. At the end of each lesson she would say, "Keep on keeping on." She inspired my love of theatre and without her, I doubt I would have had my fifty year career at the BBC.

I kept on keeping on and am grateful to Miss Firth and my mother. It's always worth listening to good advice.

Michael Rosen
Author, Poet, Presenter, Political Columnist, Broadcaster and Activist
As I came out of a forty-day induced coma, I was troubled by many different things.

I couldn't stand up, I couldn't walk, I had a tracheostomy scar that wouldn't heal, I couldn't see with my left eye, I couldn't hear with my right ear, my toes were numb, I had bouts of incontinence, my hair was falling out, my memory was failing, I had been told that I had blood clots in my pulmonary artery and microbleeds in my brain.

This was in June 2020.

I'm also someone who has experienced different kinds of trauma: the loss of my son Eddie. A chronic illness, hypothyroidism, which nearly killed me.

I have developed many strategies to deal with all these setbacks. I could pick any of them – belief in play, talk, walking, writing, being curious, going on learning and studying, co-operating with others, resistance and so on. But the simplest and easiest thing I do is what I call the "one good thing principle".

Every day, I try to do one thing – no matter how simple – that I can be proud of. When I say, no matter how simple, I mean it. It might be emptying and reloading the dishwasher rather than leaving it. Or remembering to buy my wife her favourite soup. Or replying to an email that I had been putting off. Then – this is the important bit – as I go to sleep, I focus on this one thing, breathe in-out deeply for at least a minute and smile.

I do these things every day and night.

Jasper Carrott OBE
Comedian, Actor and Presenter
Luck is when preparation meets opportunity.
The bigger they are, the harder they hit you.

Sir Anthony Seldon
Educator, Historian and Author
If you have let distance come between you and your siblings, build bridges and make peace at once.

There are a billion and one justifications or excuses given for distance, or worse. But no good justifications or excuses. Your life will improve immeasurably if you take the first steps, and so will theirs.

There is nothing sadder than siblings at war. The sooner you begin to build bridges, the easier it is.

That means now.

Steven Isserlis CBE
Cellist and Writer
I have been performing the cello core repertoire for all too many years. I realised the other day (with a rather large-limbed jolt) that this year would mark the 50th anniversary of my first performance of Dvorak's magnificent cello concerto. Doesn't make me feel young!

People often ask whether my interpretations have changed over the years. Well, of course they have – but it's often hard to describe how.

Of course, there are flashes of revelation ("why didn't I see that before?" moments); but for the most part, it is more a gradual transformation, noticing tiny details, dispensing with small irrelevancies or clichés. I liken it to one's facial features: one can look into a shaving mirror day after day without noticing any great difference; but then, one is shown a photograph of oneself (or in this case, one hears a recording of oneself) from twenty or even ten years earlier – and the change is palpable.

The good news is that in music, it is usually a positive development (at least, I hope it is); living with the music for all these years, one has had the chance to think about it more deeply, to understand it more intimately.

When it comes to the face, however – well, that's another thing.

Sir Max Hastings
Military Historian, Journalist, and Writer
The greatest gift any of us can have is to know how to be happy.

It is surprising how many rich, successful, important people miss out on this. I have always doubted that our King has it, poor man. A friend once described to me how she was walking with him around his garden at Highgrove and said "Gosh, Sir, isn't the blossom on the trees looking wonderful". He responded doubtfully: "Yes, but it will all have fallen off by tomorrow".

We need to know how to cherish the moments when good things blossom before us, taking no heed of disappointments that may lie ahead.

Both my wife and I never stop being grateful for nice things that happen, try never to take any of them for granted. One of the surest routes to unhappiness is to assume that one belongs at the front of the plane, and one of the ways of making sure of making the most of good things when they come to us is to sustain, as we do even in our late 70s, a perpetual sense of surprised joy that the ball has got over the net.

Pam Ferris
Actor
In acting, never try to be "Interesting" – rather aim to be honest. This goes for the rest of life, too.

Nigel Barley
Anthropologist
At one time I was an incorrigible paremiologist – to save you running to a dictionary that's someone interested in proverbs.

The power of proverbs lies in their being firmly rooted in human experience, a thing of nuts and bolts not abstract nouns.

Two have remained with me, dealing as they do with irrational fear and undeserved misfortune.

The first is Turkish: "A dog that has been bitten by a snake will always fear sausages".

The second is Egyptian: "An unlucky man will find bones even in a tripe supper".

Matthew Gould MBE
CEO, The Zoological Society of London

Every day, as I cycle in to London Zoo from Golder's Green, I pass numerous childhood memories, from Northways (where my grandparents used to live) to the McDonald's where my cousin had us thrown out for stamping on a Filet-O-Fish.

But the end of my ride is always the giraffes. A more incongruous sight in the centre of London it would be hard to imagine – three ladies, elegant and skittish, often peering out from the house that Decimus Burton built almost two hundred years ago.

There is invariably a small gaggle of people on the pavement, interrupting their walks or commutes to drink in the sight. The ones I can't understand are the people who walk on by, as if they hadn't just seen a giraffe. A giraffe! In central London!

The zoo is a remarkable place that holds memories for generations of Londoners. When I walk around it after everyone else has gone home, I can hear some of those memories, and the happiness they carry. Or perhaps it's just the gibbons.

Keith Leslie
Chair of the Samaritans, Leadership Mentor, Speaker and Writer

Early in my career I was taught a lesson about empathy that has stayed with me.

I worked in a competitive industry and was junior in the hierarchy. A middle-ranking manager asked for input on an issue that mattered to him, but irrelevant to what I was tasked with. I did briefly answer him, but it was the bare minimum.

Six months later, I was working on a new project where this manager – whom I had brushed off – was now the key contact. Fortunately, he seemed unconscious of my past hurried reactions, and we worked well together. He might have been gracious and ignored the past.

I always quote this as an example of the need and value of making time for people, whatever their status or your selfish interest. You never know when you will bump into someone again and your judgment on their importance will frequently be flawed. In fact, over my career I extended that thought to seek out people I knew had suffered reverses at work.

In the tough and sometimes random world of business, I observed chief executives and senior leaders who were fired or edged out of organisations, and I knew that virtually all of their usual contacts would simply delete them from their contact lists and their diaries would be empty. So, I would call them and suggest lunch and conversations about their next roles and their experiences.

With one permanent secretary, publicly fired after a scandal where he was not at fault, I made sure that I and two partners took him out to the exact same fine restaurant we took him to a few months previously.

I won lots of new business when these discarded leaders obtained new roles.

I went through this experience for myself when I was discarded and found that, although senior former colleagues were embarrassed when I got in touch, my junior colleagues had listened to my stories and took care to stay close and to encourage.

Dr Mark Porter MBE
GP and Radio Presenter

Wise people tend to spend more time listening than talking – something I have struggled with all my life. Don't make the same mistake.

Roger McGough CBE
Poet, Performance Poet, Broadcaster, Children's Author and Playwright

"Time flies" they say, but it's us that fly.
Time sits on its hands as we rush by.

In summer as hot air rises, so the days get lighter.

Time to put the clock back? Clear a space on the mantelpiece.

A suitcase becomes heavy only when lifted.

The bigger the wooden clog, the smaller the forest.

Be careful where you stop to stand and stare
Or people will stop to stand and stare at you.

To avoid jet-lag travel the day before, and remember,
By the time you get there, abroad will have moved on.

Balls of string theory are notoriously difficult to unravel.

If you have back pain, osteopaths are ideal for walking along.
Dust is the carpet of the contented.

When all is said and done
There'll be nothing left to say or do."

David Oyelowo OBE
Actor, Director and Producer
Choose gratitude over taking things for granted. There's always something to be grateful for no matter how tough things get.

Dom Joly
Comedian and Writer
Never, ever take any important decision coming off a big project. Take a break. Distance yourself. Get some perspective. Then decide. Essentially ... sleep on it.

Ali Smith CBE
Author, Playwright, Academic and Journalist
Let hope lope alongside you like the wolf we thought had died out, teeth and claws and howl and all. You thought you were alone. But there it is, so untamed that the fact it's walking so peaceably alongside you is what folk used to call a bloody miracle.

Jed Mercurio OBE
Screenwriter, Producer and Director
Take-offs are optional; landings are mandatory.

Judy Ling Wong CBE
Environmental Activist
Change is the coming together of thinking, feeling and action.

We are living in a time that requires engaged societal transformation. When we pay attention to its key drivers, we can purposefully direct change in ourselves and in others.

Research has shown that knowing what we should do does not necessarily lead to action. Motivation to act comes through our feelings. Feelings have to be nurtured through the provision of opportunities to associate emotionally with the pivotal themes that shape our lives. At the same time, strong feelings standing alone can lead to frustration and anger when it is not informed by understanding what we can do about it. So the dimension of thinking plays its role in enabling effective action once people are engaged.

Finally, action can take place only if we empower people by providing access to the structures underpinning action, with representation and engagement at its core.

Sebastian Barry
Novelist, Playwright and Poet
When I was young in the seventies maybe I thought the best advice came from Zeb Macahan in *How the West was Won*: "Never explain and never say you're sorry." Now I am officially old I realise that is the exact opposite of good advice. You had better explain yourself, because it is the path to peace; and the most generous and healing action on earth is an apology.

Harry Hill
Comedian, Presenter and Writer
If it's going badly – get off. It's going well … get off!

Suhaiymah Manzoor-Khan
Poet, Writer and Speaker

"My heart is at ease knowing that what was meant for me will never miss me, and that what misses me was never meant for me." – Imam Al-Shafii, 18th century Muslim jurist.

Thomas Harding
Author, Journalist and Documentary Maker

I am so grateful for every minute of every day.

Life can be terrible, truly terrible, but it also can be so very beautiful. Wonderful and glorious. I am thankful for every day I'm here, to share it with those I love. To be alive and still breathing. Because I can.

My nugget is to try, even though sometimes it is difficult, really difficult, and I barely have the energy or will or desire to get out of bed, but I still try to live every moment to the fullest extent. Because every second is so very, very precious.

David Kynaston
Historian and Author

One of the characters in Anthony Powell's sequence of novels, *A Dance to the Music of Time*, is a retired general. He has a seductive theory which in essence is this: given that we all have a personal myth about ourselves, however it is formed and whatever it may be, then one will just about be all right, psychologically speaking, if one can achieve a rough alignment between that myth and the objective circumstances of one's life (or at least those circumstances as perceived by oneself).

In retrospect, my own big "personal myth" moment came in 1989.

Late one afternoon, just as I was about to leave the Bedford Square offices of the publishers Chatto & Windus, the firm's legendarily straight-talking Australian head, Carmen Callil, called me into her room. We'd only met once before, and she seemed tired at the end of a long day. It took a while for her to focus, but once she did she looked hard at me and asked two questions: "So who do you want to be? Lord Muck?" By which – after some rapid mental scrabbling – I took her to mean that my choice ahead was between trying to become one of the great and the good or instead concentrating on researching and writing my books.

I forget exactly how I answered, but in the days and weeks which followed, those questions stayed obstinately in my head. I realised, in my late thirties, that how I had imagined my future self since my early twenties – as a writer of history books, operating in Grub Street outside the academy – was how I still envisaged myself. I also realised that entering middle age, there was a choice involved, a question of priorities, if I was going to make those books the very best that I could.

Some twelve years later, I read Powell for the first time, and the general's theory spoke to me strongly.

A further twenty years on, now in my early seventies and still writing history books, still not one of the great and the good (or anyway I hope not quite), I remain grateful to Carmen for the advice implicit in her questions.

But I do now realise, more than when younger, that for all sorts of reasons it is often a matter of luck – perhaps even entirely a matter of luck – whether one is able to put one's personal myth into something like practice.

All of us can, after all, only play the hand we are dealt.

Toyah Willcox
Singer, Songwriter, Actor and Televison Presenter
There are eight billion people in the world. Every single one of us is full of potential. The greatest kindness we can give another human being is to help them realise and reach that potential. Because potentially we have eight billion friends.

Nigel Planer
Actor, Writer and Musician

>If called on to speak
>At risk of pretentiousness
>I would use haikus

First, five syllables
A second line of seven
Then another five

To speak in haikus
Is, like I say, pretentious
But keeps you succinct

Richard Beard
Writer

Some years ago I wrote a squib called *The English Book of Changes*, based on the Chinese I-Ching. In search of wisdom or advice? Flip some coins and depending on heads or tails the *English Book of Changes* will provide wise guidance for any given situation.

"Make hay while the sun shines," or "one good turn deserves another". The phrases turned up by the oracle were mostly proverbs that had become clichés, but which were clichés for a reason: they were repeated because they were useful and true.

Many proverbial words of advice urge caution, or at least the ones I remember, because for me it's true that a stitch in time saves nine and that one in the hand is worth two in the bush. "Look before you leap", sure, but also be careful not to look instead of leaping. That isn't what the advice recommends.

Original words of wisdom are probably more dubious, for not yet having stood the test of time, but my dad tried his best. Cut sausages lengthways, he said, to release the heat more efficiently. Good advice but with limited applications. Another one of his, or one he wanted to pass on: "The first day of a new job is the worst. The second day is the second worst".

True, but as I get older this feels less useful on a regular basis than the best advice I have to offer, literally for specs and keys, but also in its full metaphorical glory.

If you lose something, look again in the most obvious place.

Dame Evelyn Glennie
Percussionist

My education was much more about what the school could do with the children than for us.

Doing something with others shares responsibility, decision-making and listening; doing something for another can be more one-sided and reduces the opportunity of shared curiosity and exploration.

Tim Lott
Author

When you feel down or depressed about something, simply remember that the world is constantly changing, and so are you.

I know from experience that the worst thing about depression is that it feels like it is forever – that nothing can ever get better. It is this sense of negative certainty that is so painful. But life is uncertain – always. And although that is an uncomfortable truth – especially when things are going well – it is also a great consolation when things are going poorly.

Professor Lucy Easthope
Author and Adviser on emergency planning and disaster recovery

I am an emergency planner – a role that not many people know that much about. We think about all the worst-case things that can happen, make big plans for them all, and then respond if and when they happen. It has taught me that however much we fight it, life constantly changes it and pulls that rug.

Sometimes it can be a lot.

I am constantly re-thinking my coping strategies, and if you live with me you know I don't always get them right – but here are five things I try to hold close as strategies for living in an uncertain world.

Practice the mental pirouette – focus on a point into the horizon, just like a ballerina does, when you are spinning.

Let the natural world be your balm – look for birds and buds and bulbs.

Find the words to ask for help – it gets learned out of us and so we often ask too late when the damage is done.

Laugh as much as you can. My greatest healer is a belly laugh so hard that pee comes out.

Get yourself a "go bag" – phone and crucially a phone charger, spare meds and glasses, some pants, a snack, a book, another snack. Keep it ready.

Martyn Brabbins
Conductor

My father, Herbert Henry – "Harry" – Brabbins was born in 1920, and grew up alongside his five brothers in Woodville, in the Derbyshire coalfield.

World War II came and Dad, a fit and feisty nineteen-year-old, signed up. He trained as a sniper and served throughout with 2nd Battalion, Parachute Regiment – the Red Berets.

Harry dropped into action many times, in many theatres of the conflict. He was captured at Arnhem in September 1944 and was held as a prisoner of war.

Both Harry and my mum, Enid – a land girl during the war – left school at 14 with few qualifications. My siblings, Pamela, Judith, John, Philip, and I, enjoyed a loving family environment.

After the war Harry worked as a salesman for Ratcliff Tail-lifts, travelling many miles each week. My understanding was that Harry could be a highly persuasive salesman.

One afternoon in 1968, close to Romney, near Southampton, Dad's white Vauxhall Viva was struck head-on by an HGV. Dad was cut free by the fire brigade, with multiple injuries, and after various operations he spent months in Southampton General Hospital.

From being a fit and energetic father and husband, the life-changing injuries took a heavy toll on Harry. He did return to work, although this proved to be sporadic and hard.

We went on holiday to the west of Ireland in 1973 – Dad had been awarded compensation, and he was adamant we should all enjoy some things that the money enabled him to afford.

Dad drove us all there in his green Austin Maxi, and I still recall the beauty of the Ring of Kerry, and the small town of Killorglin where we stayed in a cottage.

While we were there Dad became increasingly irritable and extremely poorly, and we had no idea of the causes. But it was clear we needed to get home to Towcester. Brother John, a novice driver, heroically got us all back.

A diagnosis of renal failure came as a terrible shock to us all. Dad received remarkable care at the Churchill Hospital, Oxford, with the giant ex-All Black rugby player, Des Oliver, as his consultant.

In due course the NHS provided home dialysis for Harry, with a mobile unit in our council house rear garden. For the rest of his life, Dad spent eight hours or so, three times each week, connected to the machine, which cleansed his blood in place of the now defunct kidneys.

Enid underwent intensive training at the Churchill Hospital, which equipped her to be Dad's nurse and carer.

Dialysis was a palaver. Lots of surgical gloves, clamps, alarms aplenty, and the smell of formaldehyde. The machine was essential. But who wants a machine for kidneys? Nobody of course, but it kept Dad alive for the next thirteen years.

Life was tough.

The strain of the responsibility had a serious impact on Enid's health, physical and mental. Dad was unable to work, so the family lived on benefits. Philip and I received free school meals. Family holidays did not happen.

My sense is that the reality of being kept alive by a machine, and having his freedom so heavily curtailed, created massive resentment and frustration for Harry. There were few things which he was able to relish in those dialysis years. Apart, that is, from his family.

I do recall some happy times chatting with Harry while he was hooked up to the machine. Although his wartime memories remained vivid, he rarely opened up about them, apart from always highlighting the incredible camaraderie he felt with his regimental companions.

I don't doubt that my dad, as a sniper, did some damage to the enemy – a troubling thing for Harry to live with, and certainly never something that he dwelt upon.

His escape during an air raid from Stalag XIIb was something he was proud of, and this did come up in our dialysis-time chats. And proud he deserved to be. Navigating with his two escapee mates by the stars – The Plough pointing the way to the North Star, walking south under cover of night and stumbling across a group of American GIs, what a relief that must have been.

A final positive thought…

I believe that being in the midst of those early dialysis years and the associated trials and tribulations helped to prepare me for the challenges of adult life.

There is much to be learnt from going through times of struggle, but it is also unwise to underestimate the scars that remain, and the healing that they may require.

Dame Shirley Bassey
Singer

Every time I walked into a theatre for my first performance of the week, I would write on the dressing room mirror, "I'm only as good as my last performance".

Enjoy your successes in life but always stay grounded.

Miranda Hart
Actor, Comedian and Writer

My favourite nugget is chicken.

Which leads me to my favourite nugget of wisdom – don't be afraid to be who you are.

I could have not said the chicken thing because it's silly and I might be judged or misunderstood, but I prefer to be as authentically myself as possible at every turn; for I believe we have all been born with a unique set of gifts and talents and a beautiful personality, that the world wants and needs in all its glory.

We exhaust ourselves pretending to be other than who we are to fit in and masking our true selves in the process. What a waste to get to the end of your life and wish you had been more yourself, said what you wanted, and followed your dreams and desires. In fact, it is rather sobering to know that that is indeed one of the top regrets of the dying.

Set yourself free, and as you become more who you are made to be and not what you should be, you will make great change, live a happier and healthier life, and give others permission to be free too.

Be vulnerable, say no when you need to, take risks, follow your dreams, look after yourself, and don't believe that the world's ways and standards are the right ways.

That still small voice within you will always be the one to follow.

Peter Brookes CBE
Cartoonist

While at school I looked on that familiar phrase, "Don't let your heart rule your head," as sound advice, but on leaving soon came to believe that the opposite was the case.

I had always preferred art as a subject to anything else, and with a passion, but the school did not offer it after O-level, and anyway my parents conventionally considered it a certain route to penury. Having failed to get into the university of my choice, I opted to become an officer cadet at RAF College Cranwell, and train to be a pilot. My father was in the RAF, I had known a forces life all through childhood and thought this was the sensible, perfectly appropriate thing to do.

I realised pretty quickly that it's a mistake to choose a career on the basis of trying to please your father, and not to be your own person.

At Cranwell I was a square peg in a round hole. I couldn't adapt to military life, hated its emphasis on uniformity over individuality, and hardly cut a dash in uniform. But worst of all, I was a completely useless pilot. Just couldn't grasp the technical skills necessary. When I realised I was the only soul in my entry who hadn't learned to drive a car, I knew the game was up. Yes, I scraped through each test on my way to flying jets solo, but as a navigator I could easily get lost. Thankfully, after two and a half years, the RAF told me to do just that before I killed myself and others.

Without hesitation I decided to apply to art college, going to Manchester then London (no better place to be in the Sixties), and have never regretted the decision for one second since.

It's what my heart told me was right, and not my head.

Elaine Paige OBE
Singer and Actor
Life is too short to waste time worrying about things you can't change. Don't look back or too far forward. Live in the moment.

Mark Emmerson
CEO City of London Academies Trust
This much I know: the pursuit of social justice and equity for the most disadvantaged children in our society through school leadership involves the relentless pursuit of an elusive and often distant objective.

Currently, school leaders face what seems to be an accelerating array of economic, political and social challenges to overcome. They are buffeted by relentless changes to expectations, guidance and regulation where many, with no experience of the reality of running schools, feel it is their right and duty to tell educators what they should be doing. They are regularly castigated and scapegoated for the ills of society and the inability to conjure up resources that simply are not there.

Nevertheless, great school leaders retain that sense of optimism, strength of purpose and sense of duty which drives schools forward. They filter, curate and protect others from the fads, vagaries and dogma that bedevil the system. They concentrate on the things that really work, creating schools that exhibit the enduring core principles of excellence in education; those being strong leadership, good behaviour, rigorous curriculum, outstanding teachers and appropriate support. They constantly wrestle with the emotionally demanding nature of the role in relation to the harrowing circumstances of some young people and the decisions they sometimes must make in balancing the interests of individuals and the many.

They do this because they care about every child they teach, their families, communities and society as a whole. Great school leaders have great ambition for their children, but keep things simple. They communicate high expectations and can mobilise committed support behind them. They are not motivated by pecuniary reward, but by the desire to create opportunities for the most disadvantaged and the reward they seek is silent. They draw satisfaction from a myriad of little things; the child who is not attending regularly coming into school, the girl with autism who now has the confidence to point out a spelling mistake in a letter, a quiet corridor, a child they have kept safe after school, and the troublesome teenager they once had to suspend who now works in their school.

This much I know: great school leaders are the architects, nurturers and protectors of all that is good in society, and we should value them more.

Mel Giedroyc
Comedian, Actor, Writer and Television Presenter
This advice I got from my darling departed dad…

If you're ever having to deal with a difficult, nasty or annoying person, simply imagine them in the nude. It really works, trust me. It humanises them and also makes them look slightly ridiculous.

It doesn't work if you're with a difficult, nasty, or annoying person in a nudist camp….

The Most Reverend Bernard Longley KC*HS
Archbishop of Birmingham
From the wisdom of Blessed Dominic Barberi, the Italian Passionist Priest who received Cardinal John Henry Newman into the Catholic Church in 1845: "I consider it should be held as a maxim that when God stirs the hearts of many to ask for any one thing it is an evident sign that He wishes to grant it".

Areeba Hamid and Will McCallum
Co-Executive Directors, Greenpeace UK

When you spend months at sea onboard Greenpeace's ships, you're lucky enough to see some incredible sights, and meet many inspiring people. But spending time away from home, in rough weather, in close quarters with your shipmates can be challenging, and so here are the best bits of advice that keep you going when it gets tough:

1. If you're in a bad mood, don't leave your cabin – you're only going to infect other people with your negativity.

2. Look up! You won't see any whales if you don't spend time looking at the sea.

Anne Hegerty
Professional Quizzer and Television Personality

There's a quiz published every year by The Mastermind Club, called The Master Quiz. If you finish in the top nine, you go on to take part in The Magnum Quiz. For years I never took part because the scores are made public. I thought, "Everyone will see how badly I've done and make fun of me."

Then in 2006 I thought to myself, "But you see these scores every year and you don't make fun of anyone. Why not just do it?"

Here's what I didn't say to myself: "Go on, have a go. You might surprise yourself. You might be better than you think."

Here's what I did say to myself: "You won't surprise yourself. You will do disastrously. And it doesn't matter. Do it anyway."

I did the quiz. I came in the top nine. In the Magnum I took a question off Egghead Kevin Ashman, probably the greatest quizzer of all time.

Two years later I made the final of the Magnum.

A year later I became a Chaser.

A year after that I won the Magnum.

It's not about thinking you might do well. It's about doing it even though you are sure to be rubbish.

" **My mother said: 'You should always buy a really good bed and a really good pair of shoes** because if you are not in one you are in the other.' "

Gloria Hunniford OBE
Television Presenter and Singer

Amanda Redman MBE
Actor

The best piece of advice I was never given but through trial and error discovered for myself is never to take people or situations at face value.

There's always a story behind every person's behaviour and understandable reasons for complex situations. The world does not revolve around me and my feelings.

Professor Marcus du Sautoy OBE
Professor of Mathematics at the University of Oxford and Author

I think I was drawn to mathematics partly because of the security it offered.

There is something reassuring about the certainty of a mathematical proof. Once you have proved something, it is there for ever. We still celebrate the mathematical discoveries of the Ancient Greeks two thousand years on. Not many other subjects can boast such longevity.

Often in times of difficulty or uncertainty in my life I have sought refuge in the perfect immutable world of mathematics. It is my safe space.

Of course for many, mathematics is far from being a refuge and is likely to instil unease and insecurity. But for me there is something amazing about creating a mathematical argument that will speak for itself, that won't need dressing up with PR, that speaks across national and cultural boundaries, that will be true for the rest of time.

That hint of immortality that a mathematical discovery can promise is an intoxicating thought.

Jasvir Singh CBE
Barrister, Social Activist and Media Commentator

My faith has always been an important feature of my identity, and it has given me great strength over the years.

The Sikh concept of "chardi kala" has helped me overcome difficult times. It's the idea of staying in exalted spirits no matter what the obstacles, and focussing on the positives even when it may seem almost impossible to find the silver lining in the cloud.

By maintaining a positive mental attitude and accepting whatever happens in my life as being part of a bigger plan, it has helped me bounce back and think clearly about what next steps I might want to take.

We will all have knockbacks in life. It's inevitable. But having that eternally optimistic outlook has allowed me to develop a resilience which means that I can look beyond the challenges immediately before me and try to focus on the better times to come.

I still have times of sadness and sorrow. Without those times, I wouldn't appreciate the bliss of contentment and happiness. But by keeping myself in a state of "chardi kala", I never feel like all is lost, and it has given me the strength and courage to carry on even in the face of great adversity.

Steph Houghton MBE
England Footballer

Never take no as an answer. Work as hard as you possibly can to get where you want to be, enjoy the challenge, there will be bumps in the road but always believe in yourself.

Professor Dame Sally Mapstone
Principal and Vice-Chancellor of the University of St Andrews

One of the lessons I have learned constantly throughout my life is that hard work is a great leveller.

It takes you places you would not have imagined you could go, it is fulfilling and satisfying, and there is no need to give it up when you get older. It is always necessary.

But hard work should not just be primarily for you; it should be for others. What you achieve and learn through working hard will afford you a more lasting happiness if its focus is getting results for other people. And when I did that becomes we did that, the sense of achievement is wide and lasting.

These days we are often told that self-care is more important than hard work. I have to disagree. Put in the hours first and then allow for the self-care. The impact on you and for others will be so much the greater, and the better.

Chris Tarrant OBE
Broadcaster and Television Personality

In my teens and early twenties my love life was always a complete shambles.

At least twice I'd lost what I believed to be the great love of my life, invariably through my own thoughtlessness, and I'd been absolutely shattered.

I'd go out on a monumental bender that lasted for days and then drip about like a wet lettuce for weeks. My whole world had come apart at the seams. There was no possible point in going on, I'd never look at another, I'd become a monk, I'd go and live in Tibet, I'd join the Foreign Legion…

And then one day I'd walk into somewhere like the chip shop and there behind the counter would be a raven-haired beauty with an irresistible smile and just a hint of vinegar and the whole silly business would start all over again.

Many years earlier I'd befriended a splendid old Gypsy lady called Peggy who lived on the banks of the River Stour just outside Wimborne. I was always welcome for a cup of tea or something stronger and one night I was chuntering on about the impermanence of all my relationships and she, wonderful wise lady that she was, put it all in a nutshell. She'd been married for over fifty years, had four great kids, and she said to me, "You're only here once, and in the end none of it matters a damn, it all comes out in the wash."

And then she told me a simple story that certainly helped me, and in later years with four daughters of my own, it certainly helped them.

Long before she'd met her husband she'd fallen madly in love with a much older man, who was married with three kids. She had gone through absolute hell over this bloke for years, sure that one day he would leave his wife and marry her, but of course he didn't, and in the end, one night he told her it was all over.

She was absolutely distraught, hysterical, in fact suicidal.

Sobbing uncontrollably, her breath coming in short gasps, she'd gone up to the top of one of the cliffs along the Dorset coastline and stood there in the wind, clenching her fists, closing her eyes and willing herself to jump. Several times she'd look down at the jagged rocks and the raging sea hundreds of feet below, and all-but summoned up the courage to let herself go. But somehow she couldn't quite will herself to step out into space. In the end she dragged herself away from the cliff's edge and went home, drowning in her own tears to begin a shattered, empty life.

"And do you know," she said, "I was thinking about it the other day for the first time in years and how close I came to ending it all – and I can't even remember his bloody name."

Professor Richard Bentall
Professor of Clinical Psychology at the University of Sheffield

Many people think that apologising for an error is a sign of defeat, but this is nearly always a mistake. Much better to think of apologising as a kind of social dance which, if executed elegantly, will smooth over the rupture in a relationship and allow social life to continue.

I have found this a useful maxim in both my personal and private life.

A corollary is: Always talk to your enemies.

Michael S Booth
Church Government Adviser, Quaker Church Affairs

Sometimes friends comment that my social media posts tend to be positive and even entertaining. That is deliberate. Life has not always been easy, but I prefer to engage with others in a way that might increase overall happiness.

Songs can be an important part of this. The Monty Python song in *Life of Brian*, "Always Look on the Bright Side of Life" brings me a smile.

How can any of us ignore the encouragement of Eric Morecambe and Ernie Wise to "Bring Me Sunshine"? After all, "In this world where we live, there should be more happiness".

There is also a call for us to live to be the best person we can be.

Matt Fishel, an LGBTQ+ musician, writes about this in his "Football Song". For those of us who aren't natural charismatic leaders, and have never naturally found a group to be part of, lines such as, "I will never be captain, but I will be King, And I'm gonna achieve the most wonderful things", and "I will never be one of the lads in the team, But I'll conquer the system and fight for my dreams, And I don't know if I could ever win, But I'm gonna be the best there's ever been," is an encouragement to be me.

The Greatest Showman song "This Is Me" is a similar call to love ourselves for who we are.

Labi Siffre's song "Something Inside So Strong" is another that inspires. I remember hearing it on a Pride march, sung by a gay men's choir outside the gates of Downing Street. It helped me know that I could make it.

We each have a chance to create a soundtrack for our lives. We have to choose our internal playlist carefully. I am lucky in that I can choose tracks that provide me with affirmation and good cheer.

Francesca Simon MBE
Writer

No-one knows what will be "useful" to them in life.

I studied Old and Middle English at Oxford, and I cannot count the number of times people asked me what possible use learning Anglo-Saxon would be. One thing I did learn was all about alliteration. I know that Horrid Henry, Perfect Peter, Moody Margaret and the rest would never have existed without my knowledge of Old English.

I've loved fairy tales and mythology since I was a child. My opera with Gavin Higgins, *The Monstrous Child*, about Hel, the Norse goddess of the dead, premiered at the Royal Opera House in 2019. Our cantata, *The Faerie Bride*, about the Welsh legend of the Lady of the Lake, has been performed at Aldeburgh and Cardiff by the BBC National Orchestra of Wales.

I think it's vital to follow your passions and interests, regardless of whether you immediately see a practical value. Unless you want to be a doctor, in which case sciences are important, or a plumber, which involves specific knowledge, study what excites you and makes you happy.

I'm currently learning to play the banjo. I am not training to be a professional musician. I just love learning to play this wonderful instrument, and look forward to my lessons every week.

Will I write about banjos? I have no idea.

Anna Williamson
Television Presenter

"If you can't get in the front door, find a way in through the back" – a saying and mantra courtesy of my darling dad who always helped me realise that in order to get my dream job, or where I wanted to be, I was to never give up at the first hurdle.

It's served me beautifully over the years as my career has gone from strength to strength.

Victoria Derbyshire
Journalist and Broadcaster

I can't remember who first said to me, "never give up". Maybe no one did. But I feel that since I was a young teenager that phrase has been part of my makeup.

In those days it involved never giving up trying to get work experience on my favourite TV show, *The Clothes Show*, on BBC 1. It took me two years of writing to the editor every single month, for him to ring me and offer me that opportunity.

I know it was in the forefront of my mind when I was diagnosed with breast cancer in 2015. For several agonising weeks while tests were carried out, I had no idea if my cancer was going to be treatable. I tried very hard to keep positive, upbeat. It wasn't always possible but I knew I wasn't ready to die. I was 46, with two young boys and an amazing partner. Never give up, keep going was what I would say to myself until the magnitude of what I was going through would overwhelm me and I would cry. Obviously with cancer I knew it wasn't in my gift. It was simply luck that the diagnosis I was given was survivable. But I always felt, rightly or wrongly, that if I had a determined approach somehow that would help me.

I now regularly say it to my children. And I hope it stays with them for the rest of their lives.

Julia Samuel MBE
Psychotherapist, Paediatric Counsellor, Writer and Speaker
I was a young therapist, inexperienced and nervous sitting opposite my client. She was inconsolable. Her first born baby girl had died at six weeks. A perfectly formed healthy baby, who had contracted a chest infection and died of pneumonia. One of those random, heartbreaking deaths we can never make sense of.

I sat powerless, unable to do or say anything that would "help her." I did the only thing I knew how to do. I listened. I asked her to tell me about her baby. She told me the depths of missing her, the presence of that child's absence in every moment of her day and through the night. Her sense of failure as a mother, her guilt. Her emptiness. Her rage. How her body hurt, her heart felt like it was breaking. I noticed that as she spoke, as her words matched her feelings, as she could feel me beside her listening to her, taking in and reflecting back the full devastation of her loss; she became calmer. I didn't stop or reduce her pain. Yet, by allowing her to express her pain, not block it, something shifted, incrementally something changed.

Over time I have learned that pain is, unfortunately, the agent of change. It is by allowing ourselves to feel the pain that we heal. The things we do to block our pain are in the end the things that do us harm, over time and sometimes through generations. But in order to bear the pain, we need support. In all its forms. Through family, friends and yes professionals like me.

When someone we love dies, it is the love of others that enables us to survive. Even, over a long time, to thrive.

Love is strong medicine.

Giles Coren
Writer, Journalist and Television Presenter
Whenever I was struggling with a homework essay or story for school, my father, who was a very famous writer and editor, used to say to me (well, he probably only said it once, but I always remembered it in a squeeze): "Whatever idea comes into your head first, throw it away, because everyone will have thought of that. And

when the next idea comes to you, throw that away too, because the bright kids will have thought of that one. Then write your third idea, because only you will have thought of that." It stood me in good stead all the way through my education and then into a career in writing and journalism and television. Originality is everything when it comes to writing and creativity, and this is a good way to ensure you have it. Although, having said that, I have passed this piece of advice on so many times over the last 25 years that I am in danger of beginning to sound very unoriginal indeed.

Paul Henderson
Crossword Setter, as Phi, Pedro, Kcit and Pangakupu
Crossword setters love putting numbers in brackets at the end of their sentences. But we all know HOPE is never just (4).

And here's another clue.

Lady is repeatedly receiving treatment, life-saving treatment (8).

That's DIALYSIS, an anagram of LADY IS IS.

Chris Mears MBE
Diver (Olympic Champion and European Champion, 2 x Commonwealth Champion, European and FINA Diving World Cup Silver Medallist and World Championship Bronze Medallist) and DJ/Producer
Success is really a repetition of passion.

Consistency builds the foundation. You cannot discredit turning up and giving your all. Passion and curiosity drives consistency – and will help you look at things differently than people around you.

Add a little patience into the mix, and you have yourself a cocktail for success.

Dr Shelley Gilbert MBE
Founder of the Charity "Grief Encounter",
Thought Leader, Activist and Influencer
Having been faced with the reality of death from the beginning of my life, orphaned by nine years old, this is some of what I've learnt the hard way. Somehow, in the world I have been brought up in, people seem to believe that if you don't talk or think about death,

it will not touch us. Yet, death is the one certainty of life. Grieve Forever. Love Forever. Love Life. Live Life.

1. *Of grief...*
   Grieving is not over in a day, week or month.

   You need time and permission to grieve, adjust and accept. Everyone does grief differently. If you learn to deal well with grief and loss, you deal well with life.
2. *Of getting through...*
   Losing someone old is sad. Losing someone young is a tragedy.

   Grief lasts forever. It is the raw, acute pain that doesn't. The difficult times are only temporary, full of ups and downs; the trick is to enjoy the ups and have courage during the downs.

   Pain is the price we pay for having loved someone, so don't fight the pain but go with it. It will lessen; think of the upward spiral of grief.

   Some days, there are things you can do. Remember, although it doesn't feel like it at the time, you are in control of your feelings. They don't control you.
3. *Of resilience...*
   You learn that the worst has happened and that you can survive. You can climb through the rubble, get through the collateral damage and keep trying.

   You need a place where you can put some words to the unsayable, thoughts to the unthinkable, feelings to the unfeelable, achieve the impossible.
4. *Of family...*
   Learning about death, struggling and suffering helps you find meaning in life.

   To me, life is about family and friendship, different kinds of love. Everything is better shared. Loneliness and isolation are the biggest battles.
5. *Of values...*
   The value statement of the charity I founded, ran and gave to our country's bereaved families is focused on caring,

kindness and compassion. I have been lucky enough to do a kindness for others every day of my life. What is a human without a heart?

"People will forget what you say or do but never how you make them feel". Maya Angelou.

6. *Of life…*
The objective actual experience of the loss is different from understanding the loss inside.

7. *Of wisdom…*
With the current information explosion, not all is reliable. Ensure you follow the right paths.

8. *Of legacy and memories…*
Meeting death so young encourages you to reflect on your own mortality and what you'd like to be remembered for and what you'd leave behind. Money and jewels for sure, but also the values of our elders and youngers.

9. *Of happiness…*
Using humour can transform anxiety. Fearing the unknown often keeps us in our old, unhelpful ways of being.

Having lost everyone he loves and living with the fear of death, Yann Martel's Pi says: "Survival had to start with me. In my experience, a castaway's worst mistake is to hope too much and do too little."

My strength has been in holding the hope that you can be happy again; knowing there's not only light at the end of the tunnel but also more lights to behold. One candle can light many lights.

Painful and tough as it has been, I'd still choose the way I've travelled through life. Regrets, I have a few, but I did it my way.

Brad Hall
Olympic Bobsledder (1 x European Champion and 1 x World Championship Silver)
The quotation: "Tough times never last, tough people do," defines a lot of what I've gone through as an athlete and as a person.

Having the discipline to keep focused on your goals or even just to keep moving forward to stop the difficult times from getting the better of you shows resilience, and that you still have faith that better times are coming.

Some people may have to endure long periods of suffering, upset or disappointment but it's ultimately those that never give up hope and never stop trying who are successful, whether in sport, work or happiness.

Devoting yourself to a goal or cause is extremely powerful. It gives you stability even in uncertain or troubling times and that's what's helped me navigate through my challenges and come out the other side stronger.

Jools Holland OBE
Musician, Composer and Television Presenter

I'm flattered to be asked to contribute a nugget of wisdom. I really am not sure if I have the right qualifications to give out good advice. In fact, one guru said to me, "The beginnings of wisdom start with the knowledge that you don't know everything".

I have learned in my life that people we meet and pass by all have their own story to tell. Therefore it's always good to give people a chance, because you never know what's happening in the background of their lives.

The other thing I've learned is, it's perhaps wiser to try to understand rather than judge people.

When a young actor asked Laurence Olivier for some tips on having a long and successful career, the great actor told the young man, "Don't get in trouble with the tax people".

My advice to young musicians would be, to quote Mary Lou Williams, "Love the music you play, love the people you're playing it with and the people you're playing it to".

On a more practical note, if you're building a recording studio, remember to put in air conditioning, because all those electrical devices make it quite hot.

Hope this is of some help, and remember there are no problems, merely opportunities.

Professor Simon Shorvon
Consultant Neurologist and Emeritus Professor of Clinical Neurology
The book is not going to die.

A growing cacophony of voices has, in the last 20 years, predicted the death of the book. It was confidently assumed that the printed page would be swept away by the information tidal wave that is the internet and by all of its white horses: Kindles, ebooks, blogs, information repositories and such like. But the book has endured, and indeed is thriving, and no doubt will continue to do so – and this is a cause of celebration.

No electronic media shares the feel and the visual delight of a book, the enjoyment of handling, the rustle of page turning or the appeal of ownership. No electronic media can mimic the pleasure in entering a library, and the indulgence of browsing shelves.

But survival is more than simply a matter of aesthetics.

Information on the internet is often anonymous, false and unreliable. It has no quality control, and no editors or publishers providing oversight.

The book on the other hand is, at its best, a well-crafted object conveying the authority, the reasoned argument and the art of its author. A good book is a subtle object to savour slowly and at length. Its text will have taken time to consider and to write, and the best books have distilled lifetimes of thought. Electronic material in contrast is by its nature often hurried and thoughtless, with the emphasis on form not content.

At its core though, the good printed book – with its long gestation, its authority, its aesthetic, its subtlety and its durability – will surely outlast all other methods of communication.

Think of the contribution of books to human civilisation and to human endeavour and pleasure, and shudder at the thought of a world without books. The demise of the book does not bear human contemplation.

Tim Winter
Academic, theologian and Islamic scholar
"Humanity left to itself, its life drained of spiritual significance, follows

the false doctrine of the survival of the fittest, represses its painful sense of exile, and enters gradually and unconsciously into darkness. Lacking a true center of gravity, human beings then experience upon this earth the eruption of the Inferno, with consequent moral devastation. Sufism is the alternative current in history, even the secret essence of history. Sufi science, which is disconcerting to those who are attached to rational dialectic, is an unveiling of Divine Grace, which exists everywhere, always, in all hearts. This subtle science, which refuses to incarcerate the Holy Spirit in formulas, calls humanity to enter consciously the field of universal brotherhood and sisterhood and to look upon physical nature as an open book of spiritual symbols. Sufism plants its inspiring message in hearts full of nostalgia for revelation – for a true paradigm, for a spiritual language that could replace the analytic, technical, didactic and manipulative language of the world. The living words of a Sufi master, who is devoted passionately to the service of Divine Beauty, must be of an order distinct from all theology and philosophy, must be the opposite pole of all ideology."
(Lex Hixon Nur Al Jerrahi, *Atom from the Sun of Knowledge*, Westport CT: Pir Publications, 1993, pp.327-328.)

Professor Jim Al-Khalili OBE
Theoretical Physicist, Author and Broadcaster

I have been lucky in my life. I know that some people will say arrogant things like, "I make my own luck", or that, "it's funny how the harder I work, the luckier I seem to get," suggesting that success in life is not down to luck at all. Nevertheless, I have been lucky, both in the choices I have made and in the paths I have found myself on through no action on my part.

As an established scientist, I teach, I carry out research in wonderful subjects like quantum physics and the nature of space and time, I write, I make TV and radio programmes, I give talks about my work, and I then get patted on the back for doing such a jolly good job. But the truth is, I have been lucky … lucky enough to pursue my passion and to continue enjoying what I do.

But as I enter my, how shall I put it, senior years, I find that I am increasingly at peace with the world.

I know we live in difficult times and face so many challenges, and I often feel guilty that I have been blessed with a wonderful, loving family, health and happiness, when so many people don't have these things. But I will say something about what my scientific training has given me that I am grateful for, and that is confidence in a world that is comprehensible.

By this I don't mean that everything that happens is rational and logical and can be understood, but that there is cause and effect, that even when random or unexpected events happen, such as terrible natural disasters or being struck down by deadly illnesses, there is still a rational reason behind how and why they happen.

I am not religious, so I don't mean there is a grand plan laid out by a supernatural designer, but rather that there is, somewhere, an explanation for everything, even if we don't have it, and even though we often do not have control over events that affect us.

Still, the universe is comprehensible and I like that, even if I do not comprehend it. But I'm trying.

Lily Ebert MBE
Holocaust Survivor

The most important message I can give is never in your life give up hope.

I was in the worst of places, Auschwitz-Birkenau, where the Nazis killed my mother and youngest brother and sister. I lived in fear that I would not survive each day. Yet here I am at the age of ninety nine, with a large and loving family. At that time I could never have imagined that I would survive let alone thrive with my family. Not losing hope helped me get through each horrific day in the camp.

My second message is always be kind. It doesn't matter if someone is different to you. No one is better or worse than someone else. We are all only different. Appreciate the differences and the world will be a much nicer place to live.

Justin Webb
Journalist and Broadcaster

Put up with stuff... This is easy for people to say who have very little to put up with, but my early and very unhappy life, fatherless, deeply affected by mental illness, could have been a place of pain with long term consequences but instead became a place of learning to cope: to be resilient. And that is a good thing. Life can be pretty grim. Learn to enjoy what you can and cope with what you cannot.

I'm not exactly suggesting the stiff upper lip of yesteryear but a refusal to dwell on sadness is part of the solution to it.

Sebastian Faulks CBE
Novelist, Journalist and Broadcaster
Take your work seriously. Leave no stone uncrossed, no "t" undotted, no extra mile unsprinted. Fight to the death for every syllable and every atom. It's all you have and all you leave.

But don't take yourself seriously. You're a hapless fool, like the rest of us, trapped in a cosmic joke of which we alone among creatures know the ending. Understanding this, and sharing that knowledge in laughter, is the basis of all friendship – and of most of Shakespeare. People who take themselves seriously have only one use: to be laughed at by the rest of us.

Pray. What have you got to lose?

If when travelling you see a great place for lunch, don't think it's too early and that you'll find somewhere better in half an hour. You won't. Book in, have a drink first, take your time ordering and it's one o'clock before you know it.

You can't go wrong with Cotes du Rhone.

Dr Jim Down
Consultant in Critical Care and Anaesthetist, UCLH NHS Foundation Trust
I have always been anxious.

There has always been something on the horizon to worry about, ever since I did weekly French vocabulary tests as an eight year old. Each test was followed by 24 hours of carefree bliss, before the next one elbowed its way into my consciousness.

As I got older the list of things to fret about grew to include school bullies, puberty, potential girlfriends, O levels, A levels, career choices, Catholicism, university finals, alcohol consumption, professional dilemmas and mistakes, my parents' health, climate change and finally the big one, my own health.

In some ways the anxiety has served me well. Driven by fear of failure, I have worked hard and passed far more exams than I have failed. I have also, so far, avoided a major disaster at work, stayed fit (partly to reduce the grounds for hypochondria) and treated others well (partly to avoid guilt and its associated anxiety).

But then a difficult case at work pushed me over the edge. My anxiety spiralled out of control and I had to pause and re-examine everything.

My problem was uncertainty. I was spending too much time trying to eradicate it by continuously scanning the future for the next potential hazard. I kept telling myself that if I could just get past this booby trap, then I'd be able to relax.

But I couldn't, of course, because there was always something new to worry about.

So now I'm trying to accept uncertainty. I don't like it, but I am learning to live with it and these are the nuggets that help me – most of the time...

Don't investigate any physical symptom for at least five days (unless it is immediately life threatening). By then most have mysteriously disappeared.

Manage the symptoms of your anxiety. I use cold water swimming and regular exercise. Both clear my head and help me sleep.

When you are worrying, you could be living. It's impossible to do both at once.

Try not to regret. We all make mistakes. Apologise and move on.

Accept that everything in life is a compromise. Everything.

Sir Brendan Foster CBE
Athlete, Television Commentator and Race Organiser (European and Commonwealth Champion, 1 x Commonwealth Silver, 1 x Olympic Bronze, 1 x European Championship Bronze and 1 x Commonwealth Bronze)
In 2017 after 37 years of commentating on athletics for the BBC including nine Olympics and even more World Championships, Great North Runs and London Marathons, I decided it was time to retire.

I'd had a great innings and it was time for another challenge.

My long-time friend and colleague John Caine asked if I fancied joining him to walk the famous Camino de Santiago.

Known in English as The Way of St James, it is a pilgrimage to the shrine of the apostle James in the Cathedral of Santiago de Compostela in Galicia in north western Spain.

The Camino is a UNESCO World Heritage site and attracts thousands of pilgrims every year. The eight hundred kilometre route takes about four weeks, and about twenty five kilometres of walking every day.

The journey from St Jean Pied de Port to Santiago de Compostela is a hugely enjoyable walk. I shared mine with Eric Wilkins, a colleague of thirty plus years, as well as fellow international athlete and Olympic medallist Ian Stewart; all captained by John, our Camino manager. We all agreed that John was the star of our little show.

A highlight for me was a conversation with an eighty-five-year-old Belgian called Ptolemy.

He was sitting with his wife at a coffee stop in the hot sun, three quarters of the way to our destination at the top of a really tough incline, as I joined them for a drink. We looked a rather tired elderly group.

I asked him why he was doing the Camino. He paused for a moment and answered, "I'm eighty five, and I've decided that I'd rather die with memories than die with dreams".

That's my memory of a wonderful few weeks walking across Spain in the sunshine with a group of friends and taking with me the thoughts from a wise old man with a wise old name.

Jonathan Dimbleby
Television and Radio Presenter, Author and Historian
I find this a great source of balm. It is from William Blake's *Auguries of Innocence*. It is a wonderful poem.

> "To see a World in a Grain of Sand
>   And a Heaven in a Wild Flower
>   Hold Infinity in the palm of your hand
>   And Eternity in an hour".

Dr Gee Walker MBE
Charity Founder

In 2005 my son Anthony Walker, who was eighteen, was waiting at a bus stop with his mixed-race cousin and a white girl.

As they waited they were racially abused by a white person on the opposite side of the road, so they decided to walk away from the antagonist to protect each other from the situation. In so doing the bus came along but failed to stop so they ran across to the park with the intention to get ahead of the bus.

The abuser then recruited his friends, drove ahead, ambushed, attacked and killed my beautiful son.

Our entire human functionalities collapsed and came crashing down around us like a tornado from hell. My first thought was – how can anyone survive this enormous loss?

Loss is not foreign to me. I have experienced grief before, however, nothing on God's Earth prepared me for the loss of my boy.

I soon recollected that Anthony has siblings, a father, nieces, nephews, a beloved grandma, family, friends and the community who would be affected by the loss.

I have got to survive because this pain of loss is not exclusive to me. I realised that I must survive for all of the above and more. I needed something bigger than myself. I needed to focus on others rather than my consuming pain of absence.

I made the decision to forgive Anthony's killers, because of that great untainted love for my child, my own peace of mind, my strong faith and obedience to God and furthermore, the fact that hate, anger, the need for revenge and bitterness are contributing factors which result in loss and harm to innocent lives.

Experiencing the pain of grief, I realised there are no grief quick-fix solutions.

I am not ashamed to show my emotions.

I cry and pray, pray and cry some more when I miss my boy.

I will talk about Anthony unashamedly until the day I die by establishing a lasting legacy in his name.

Duke McKenzie MBE
Boxer (3-Weight World Champion: IBF Flyweight, WBO Bantamweight and WBO Junior-Featherweight)

I could never have reached the levels of success that I did in my career had it not been for my elder brother Dudley, who had wisdom beyond his years.

I wish you could have met him.

The best piece of advice he gave me was: "Sometimes you have to ride off someone else's confidence until yours kicks in. I've got your back."

Had my brother not been in my corner for my British, European and World title fights I would never have succeeded. Had he told me to climb Mount Everest or fight Mike Tyson I'd have done it. I had that much faith in him.

All that I am or will ever be is because of Dudley.

Toby Porter
CEO of Hospice UK

A lifetime working in the charity sector has taught me many lessons, and if not wisdom I've certainly learnt a deep appreciation for human kindness and our ability to help each other.

As a former CEO of Acorns children's hospice and now CEO of Hospice UK some people might assume work concerned with death and dying is depressing. Undoubtedly I have heard many a heartbreaking story along the way. But it's the courage, compassion and generosity I've experienced which has made this work a privilege.

The thread of wisdom running through it all is that we need to be able to speak openly about death, dying and bereavement. They touch all of our lives in some way, yet all too often the taboo around these conversations can leave people feeling isolated. It's important that we all know what it means for us and our loved ones to be in a good place to die – physically, emotionally, financially, spiritually, and crucially, with the right care and support in place.

It's why I'm so proud of the brilliant, compassionate care delivered by our hospices who help people die with dignity, and why I'm so proud of the Hospice UK's Dying Matters campaign which tackles some of the toughest conversations around death, dying and grief.

Talking about dying helps us to live better, and living life to the fullest is wisdom we can all agree on.

Graeme Garden OBE
Comedian, Actor, Author, Artist and Television Presenter
If somebody congratulates you or says they admire something you have done or said or created, don't deflect their praise with a shrug, saying, "Oh it was nothing". You would seem to be questioning your admirer's taste. Accept the compliment and say, "Thank you".

Give your admirer the pleasure of knowing that you enjoy their appreciation.

Professor James Appleby CBE
Psychiatrist, Lead of the National Suicide Prevention Strategy for England
What is the most fascinating part of working with other people, especially on something important like health? That their opinions are different to your own. That they have looked at the same facts, with the same good intentions, and come to a different conclusion.

Every point of view benefits from challenge.

Avoid the echo chamber.

Alison Bloxham
Therapy Lead, Transplant Sport
Having been involved in Transplant Sport for over twenty years I have come to realise that life is precious and that good health is the biggest gift we can receive.

I have been lucky enough not to suffer serious illness, disability or health challenges. But I see how fragile a stroke of fortune this is when I see people who have had ill health and near-death experiences, forcing them into life-changing experiences.

But here's the thing – instead of bemoaning their bad luck they embrace the challenge, push their limits, live life to the full and celebrate their second chance at life to the max.

Whenever I go to the Transplant Games all the problems, pressures and stresses I may have felt are reduced to the trivial status that they deserve. I am buoyed by the athletes' incredible optimism and zest for life. It is like taking an appreciation drug for all the positives in life and cannot help but uplift you.

The athletes talk about the fact that just being alive and on the start line is as good as winning a gold medal. In no other sports-related therapy jobs have I worked with athletes who are as supportive of each other and appreciative of all the help they get to achieve what, for most, would be modest goals.

Life is to be lived to the full; it doesn't matter what level you are at. Just having good health to enjoy whatever you do means you have won gold.

Go and celebrate.

Nina Wadia OBE
Actor and Comedian

In an interview I was asked what has been my greatest achievement. I instinctively said, being a mother, and then added, being a wife … and then stopped.

Later that evening, I thought, how unusual, I said nothing about my career. This bothered me for a few days. So I decided to meditate on it. I imagined my life as climbing a mountain, because I was ambitious when I was younger and wanted to achieve certain goals and milestones.

Every time I succeeded and got to the top, all there was, was another mountain to climb. However, when I looked back, I saw all my family and friends cheering me on.

I realised then, I don't want to strive so hard any more. I want to appreciate the journey and everyone who has been on it with me instead.

Judith
Listening Volunteer, Harrow Samaritans

Never mind, "Location, location, location".
Never mind, "Education, education, education".
The most important thing is, "Communication, communication, communication".

IMAGINE ALL YOUR TERRORS HAVE COMBINED AND TAKEN PHYSICAL SHAPE.

GIVE THIS MONSTER A NAME.

NOW IMAGINE THAT IT'S NO MORE THAN SEVEN CENTIMETRES HIGH AND YOU'RE DROPPING IT INTO A BLENDER.

Andy Riley
Author, Cartoonist and Screenwriter

Steve Punt
Comedy Writer, Comedian and Actor

Somebody once said, "Find a job you love doing and you'll never have to work a day in your life."

I say "somebody" because when I Googled to check the source it suggested Mark Twain, Mark Antony and Confucius – as well as someone called Unknown.

I think that means that nobody actually has a clue who said it. But no-one likes admitting that they don't know.

If more people were willing to admit when they don't know things, the world would be a better place – except for doctors.

Doctors are the last people you want to admit they don't know things. What you want a doctor to say is, "Ah yes, I recognise these symptoms. And here is how we treat them." You do not want a doctor to scratch their head and say, "Well, I'm baffled. No idea what this is. Has it always been purple?"

Val Garland
Make-up Artist

Marilyn Monroe: "Imperfection is beauty, madness is genius and it's better to be absolutely ridiculous than absolutely boring."

The Rt Hon. Lord Heseltine
Politician and Businessman

People ask me about their choice of career. I cannot answer this question without knowing anything about them. I can give one piece of advice: "Do something that enables you to look forward to Monday morning".

Etta Murfitt MBE
Dancer and Choreographer

Breathe, be brave and you will get through it.

One second, one minute, one hour, one day. You will get through it, sometimes fearing the journey and sometimes enjoying the ride.

With courage we get there in the end.

Breathe. Embrace. Dive in.

Jonathan Pearce
Football Commentator

Always be true to yourself and be the best that you can be.

Aim for the stars.

You may need to adjust those aims over time but never sell yourself short. Believe in yourself especially when you think others seem to have lost their belief in you. Be loyal and loving to those who matter to you and to whom you matter.

Fill your life with joyous noise but also learn to enjoy the silences.

Gaby Roslin
Television Presenter

My parents always told me to follow my dreams.

They used to say don't ever give up, but never hurt anyone along the way and treat everyone the same.

I now say the same to my daughters. I just wish for them to be happy and believe they can fulfil those dreams as I think everyone can.

Stay kind, keep being positive and always spread joy.

Professor Amia Srinivasan
Philosopher, Chichele Professor of Social and Political Theory at the University of Oxford.

'Tell me, what is it you plan to do
With your one wild and precious life?'
Mary Oliver, *The Summer Day*

Steve McClure
Rock Climber and Writer

Follow your heart for the sweetest taste of success.

Strawberries. This is the name of a rock-climbing route in north Wales near the village of Tremadog. One of the most famous routes in the history of British climbing, the quality and difficulty have become legendary. It was first climbed in 1980, first with a lot of practice and rests on the rope, and then at last, a clean ascent with no falls or resting on the equipment.

Strawberries follows a thin, finger-width crack splitting an overhanging wall. It's fifteen metres long, but begins from a small ledge after forty metres of already difficult climbing. The route feels way up in the sky. Hanging over the road, it is visible for every passer-by. It is the symbol of hard climbing.

This route has always been in my mind. At ten years old, Strawberries had just been climbed, just as I found myself falling in love with the sport. Poring over the headlines and pictures in magazines is my first memory of the world of extreme rock. They stayed with me, they stayed with everyone from that generation. New routes came along, harder ones, but Strawberries remained king.

I went to the area many times. We'd stare up in awe, with Strawberries towering above, always well out of my league.

Ascents of the route were few and far between, with every climber falling off, and taking a number of attempts before success. Sometimes many attempts, perhaps spread over days, or weeks, or months.

The first "on-sight" ascent was in 1987 by world champion climber Stefan Glowacs. This is the ultimate style of climbing; to climb from bottom-to-top first attempt, with no information or practice.

This ascent was way ahead of its time, and it took another 24 years for the next repeat in this style from Jorg Verhoeven. The on-sight was the challenge.

I waited for the right time, saving it for an on-sight effort, waiting for everything to fall perfectly into place. But suddenly I crossed a threshold and realised my time was running out. I watched as years went by without even getting a chance; too much rain, too much work, too injured. I didn't even get to the cliff. I just wanted to do it, even if I fell, what did it really matter compared to never trying? To leave Strawberries un-tried would be my greatest failure.

And then suddenly an opportunity – a few days free from work, a partner, good weather, and a camera team ready to capture my efforts. It would surely make a great film, the exposure, the immense backdrop, the story and the battle which was surely guaranteed. Everything was set – times, teams, story-line, even clothing choice.

We arrived a day early, just myself and climbing partner, to try easier routes and get a feel for this amazing place. And suddenly there I was, staring up at Strawberries from the road as I had done so many times before.

It was dry and clean, the air was clear and fresh and a light breeze drifted over the cliff. Conditions were perfect. My chance was now. There could be no waiting.

But what of the camera team, the film, the story?

What of it?

Why was I really there? To make a film, to capture my efforts for the world to see?

No, this was about my challenge, me versus the route, a dream for so long. Sometimes you have to follow your heart, and to know when the time is right. Trust your judgement, know yourself and know what is really important. Seize the moment when it comes.

And so I began, stepping out onto the first hard moves, already forty metres above the ground, the exposure shocking me as I tried to stay focussed. At first I climbed awkwardly, out of rhythm, missing the efficiency; burning precious energy. What if I did fall? So what. I'll do it next go, or after a few tries. That would still be lovely, still a childhood dream. It won't matter either way. All I have to do is give it my best shot, and my best shot is now. Calmer, I find myself in the zone, moving fluidly, seeing what the rock has to offer. I can feel the texture of the rock, the bite of friction into my skin. It's desperate, and yet it's easy … and suddenly it's over, good handholds and the top is within reach.

The dream is reality.

That feeling was immense, a feeling of satisfaction for climbing such a test-piece in good style, but far more, for climbing so well, keeping it together, taking the chance, and knowing that today was really the day.

Dr Musharraf Hussain OBE
Scientist, Educator and Religious Scholar

Recently I bumped into Haji, an old friend I consider a successful parent.

I reflected on his success, and this is what I remember of our time together at his home: he spoke gently and respectfully to his children. The gentleness was his hallmark. He always listened carefully to them, encouraged them and then offered advice.

So, what was the consequence of such gentle behaviour?

All his six children turned out to be successful: a director of public health, a dentist, an accountant et cetera. The principle I learnt is that people tend to become what the most important person in their lives thinks of them.

For his children, Haji was the most important person, since he regarded them as important and respectable. Lo and behold, they turned into respectable and important people. The lesson is we must think the best, believe the best and express the best about others.

"Blessed Prophet, we sent you as a witness, giver of good news and a warner, invite to your Lord since you are a shining lamp. Give good news to the faithful that they will have a great bounty from the Lord". (*The Quran*, 33:45)

Emma Rice
Actor, Director and Writer

When I was at drama school I invited my old teacher to see me play Titania. I did my hair, put glitter on my face and performed with serious grace. After the show, I pranced up to receive my praise. She said, "You looked lovely – but were a little boring".

I was mortified but, with hindsight, it was the best thing she could have said. I think of it always when I am making work and it propels me to make brave, unglamorous and unusual choices.

So my advice is simple. Don't be boring.

John Richards
President, Atheism UK

Ignorance is not bliss.

Wouldn't you rather know whether a previously unseen snake that's crossing your path is venomous, or delicious when barbecued?

Survival has favoured suspicion towards the unfamiliar. The quicksand of ignorance and doubt is scary, consequently we crave certainty. Unfortunately, only one thing is absolutely certain and that's that everything will change.

Why is this?

It's because our universe contains time.

Time is an unstoppable conveyor belt, a continuous procession of alterations. Having no static instants means that nothing can retain its "original" properties, its identity.

This makes truth subjective, provisional and temporary until the end of time.

Perhaps we shouldn't be dogmatic.

Nicholas Owen
Television Presenter and Journalist

Out of the blue, with no symptoms, a routine check-up in 2002 showed a tumour on my right kidney. Back then, a full nephrectomy – removal of the affected organ – was basically the only treatment. I was so lucky that the cancer had not spread.

It was decision time when it came to how to approach the rest of my life. I was a TV news presenter. Not an especially secure occupation. Telling the world I'd had cancer might affect my work prospects.

I decided anyway to share my story with anyone interested. So for more than a dozen years, I was proud to be a Patron of Kidney Cancer UK, spreading the word about what help was available to others who found themselves in my situation.

The most important thing, I have always thought, is to be able to share feelings, fears and experiences with others in the same, inevitably scary boat.

Danny Sebastian
Antiques Dealer and Television Presenter

1. Without commitment you'll never start, but more importantly without consistency you'll never finish.
2. It's only when the well runs dry that we truly appreciate how precious the water was.

Jane Green
Writer, Founder and Chief Content Officer, Emerald Audio

The key to happiness is not getting what you want, but wanting what you have got.

Whenever I have thought that reaching a goal would make me happy, I merely end up moving the goalposts once I have got there.

I've spent years understanding the concept that life is where you look; life has a tendency to throw all kinds of curveballs at you, but how you deal with those curveballs is entirely up to you.

Jenny Eclair
Comedian, Actor and Novelist

Plant tulip bulbs in September, you will be grateful in March.

If in doubt, handwash.

Be careful on Twitter.

In your sixties you will need a sturdy pair of toe-nail clippers. Be careful that the clippings don't ping back into your eye. Goggles are a good idea.

Going to the dentist once every ten years is not enough and if your teeth are yellow, red lipstick makes them look worse. Try a plum or raspberry shade.

Before you sit down on holiday, make sure you're not about to break your sunglasses.

Draw and paint, even if you can't draw or paint.

Sometimes you will think you're having a heart attack, because you ate your tea too fast. On the other hand don't jump to the conclusion that you have indigestion when in fact you are having a heart attack. Life can be tricky.

Being late is rude.

Be nice to waiters.

Try to remember how many glasses of wine you've had.

Don't forget to use sun-screen.

Always finish the course of antibiotics, unless you happen to be allergic to them.

Evan Davis
Journalist, Economist and Presenter
One problem at a time.

During the pandemic, my husband Guillaume and I found ourselves watching a rather apocalyptic Belgian sci-fi series called *Into the Night*.

The implausible premise was that the Sun was suddenly emitting deadly rays which had killed almost everybody on earth. Any exposure to daylight was fatal. However, there were a small number of survivors who were lucky to be on a hijacked plane which had flown away from the danger of daylight into the dark of night. But the challenge for the passengers and crew was that they now had to endlessly race against the sunrise by flying west to stay in the dark.

In the series, they had problems. Many problems. Landing, refuelling and taking off before dawn for example. But one phrase that kept being repeated as they tried to deal with multiple scrapes was, "one problem at a time".

The message of course was that they had to think straight, deal with the hazards in a structured way; not allowing themselves to become frazzled by the cacophony of different alarms signalling peril.

That phrase "one problem at a time" seeped into the consciousness of Guillaume and I. We started using it with increasing frequency whenever too many things were going on at the same time. I'm talking here of mundane things rather than the life-threatening adventures of the folks in *Into the Night*. Things like, the printer getting jammed, the dog clamouring for his meal, and a neighbour wanting help with something. Reciting "one problem at a time", we began to discipline ourselves to focus on one thing, then move on. Focus again, and move on.

As it turns out, this policy of rigidly dealing with one problem at a time turns out to be incredibly helpful – a way of imposing mental order in those moments where numerous concerns are all crowding into one's head, making it hard to think straight about any of them.

By dispensing with one item in the catalogue of concerns, you put yourself on the right track and give yourself the strength to deal with the next one.

Guillaume and I have each become devotees of this approach. But most significantly, I've found it useful not just for those busy evenings where there is too long a To Do list; it's also an approach to managing and controlling your feelings in a stressful period of life. I always find it psychologically liberating to itemise the different things that are contributing to the stress or anxiety, and to solve them as far as possible (or at least to reflect on them) individually.

I know it's the opposite of multi-tasking. But then, most of us find single-tasking hard enough.

Colin Thackery
Chelsea Pensioner, War Veteran, Singer
and Winner of Britain's Got Talent, 2019

Having lost my beloved wife of sixty six years, I was at a low ebb. I applied to be accepted into The Royal Hospital Chelsea and was admitted as a pensioner in 2017. I settled in to life at RHC and wore my scarlet coat with pride to many functions, but I was unfulfilled because singing was not part of my life at that time. I have sung all of my life and, apart from entertaining with a friend after the monthly curry evening, did very little else.

After one of the curry sessions I was approached by another pensioner who reminded me that I had mentioned that "if you don't use it you will lose it" and singing was certainly one of them. He suggested that I have a go at entering for Britain's Got Talent. I said that was a daft idea at my age – I am now ninety two – but he said, "I dare you!"

Never one to refuse a challenge, I submitted the application that evening.

The rest is history as they say, because I went on to win and have not stopped singing since. This was all in 2019 and life has changed beyond all recognition.

Jack Isaac
His Majesty's Prison and Probation Service

'Smooth Seas Do Not Make Skilful Sailors.'

Samantha Renke
Actor

Dream and dream big.

If that speckle of doubt starts to creep in that says you aren't doing enough, aren't pushing yourself enough then stop and take a breath and remember simply this: If you do one thing each day no matter how big or small you will arrive at your destination.

Having a disability means that I don't always feel like my body works as I'd hope, or that the world sees my potential, so I decided a long time ago to be kind to myself. Each day I did something to get me closer to where I wanted to be even if it was sending a simple email or opening up a Twitter account, to the bigger things like going for an audition or writing a book.

Be kind to yourself and remember that old saying, "Rome wasn't built in a day."

Why would you ever expect that your own path wouldn't need the time and attention to come to pass just in the same way?

Dharmesh Sheth
Journalist

Be nice. Don't burn any bridges. Make lots of contacts. You never know when you will need them.

Philippe Sands KC
Writer and Lawyer

Words and music make a difference.

The lines I most often come back to were written in 1992, but the origins go back even further, as the poet Leonard Cohen liked to take time with his craft.

The poem, or song, is titled Anthem.

The lines are in the form of a refrain, they repeat.

> Ring the bells that still can ring
> Forget your perfect offering
> There is a crack, a crack in everything
> That's how the light gets in

Lines of encouragement. Lines that invite us to keep to that which is right. Lines that tell us not to lose hope.

Harry Mount
Writer, Journalist and Editor of "The Oldie"
Do everything in life you can to suppress your ego.

The overblown ego leads to grandness, grumpiness, showing-off and being boring. The suppressed ego leads to curiosity, kindness, being good company and asking questions.

My model in these affairs has been the late Bill Deedes, who I worked with at the Telegraph when he was in his nineties and I was in my thirties. He'd won an MC, edited the *Telegraph* and been a Cabinet Minister – yet he never showed off; he was never grumpy; he always looked forward, never backwards. He always filed early with exactly the right number of words. He never said no to anything. No wonder he was still working when he died at 94, loved by all.

Griff Rhys Jones OBE
Comedian, Writer, Actor and Television Presenter
I am constantly scanning the Saturday newspapers and finding out how to live forevermore.

Squats, highly coloured berries, eight hours sleep: that sort of thing. But there was one simple instruction from a fitness guru that I did adopt. That is to stand on one leg while brushing your teeth. Apparently it improves your balance. And I had noticed that my balance in my sixties was distinctly less assured. So, every day I saw away on one leg, and then change to the other and saw some more. I don't know about strengthening my ankles, but I can say that I am now really good at brushing my teeth on one leg – a self-satisfying solitary geriatric skill.

Dr Martin Shaw
Author, Mythologist and Oral Storyteller
From the mind of the poet Gary Snyder:
"Do not be a slave to your lesser talents. Take courage. It is fine

to dream big, but in the end the making of the work itself is the deepest reward. Get in contact with that essential joy, whatever your work may be, and all will be well."

Randeep Singh Lall
Deputy Lieutenant for Greater London.
The three cardinal questions one must ask oneself are:
Where am I from?
What is my purpose?
Where will I be going?
Ok, so one needs to think here, if one has come from somewhere, what did one bring?
Ok, now whatever one brought determines one's existence today.
So what does one need to take with one? Which then becomes one's purpose.
One can take service of humanity.
One can take good deeds.
One can take spiritual currency in the form of meditation.
Sometimes we sit and talk about the good old days.
In ten years' time, we will sit again and talk about the good old days.
Embrace the moment of now as the good old day. Live for the second, the moment, the hour, the day.
Embrace the here and now as if tomorrow may not come.
    After all, tomorrow may not come.

Denise Welch
Actor, Writer, Broadcaster and Television Personality
"Comparison is the thief of joy," is a favourite quote of mine.

Too often in this day of Instagram perfection we find ourselves comparing our lives with others. Everyone appears to be richer, more glamorous, more successful, happier, the list goes on. But in reality everyone is fighting their own battles.

The more people profess to have a perfect life the unhappier they often are deep down.

As a sufferer of depression I look at some photos of myself taken during a bad episode. Anyone who didn't know my suffering would think I was happy.

I try to no longer compare my life to others. I try to end every day grateful for what I have. I try not to judge other people who hurt me, but to understand why they have behaved that way.

Age has many downsides but the older you become you learn that if your problems were in a pile next to a million other people's, you'd choose your own.

Jim Carter OBE
Actor
I don't regret anything that I've done. I only regret those things that I haven't done.

Professor Chris Stringer CBE
Physical Anthropologist
Even a journey of a thousand miles begins with one step

I think I first heard these words as a teenager, quoted by Mao Zedong, but I now know they originated from the Chinese philosopher Lao Tzu.

I haven't been confident in my abilities (I now know that to be Impostor Syndrome) and they have helped me whenever I was faced with seemingly insurmountable tasks, such as doing my PhD in Bristol, or being forced to head up a divisional restructuring.

Now I quote those words to people who say that one person (them) eating less meat or flying less miles is never going to help fight the huge threat of climate change.

Anne Mayer Bird and Catherine Mayer
Authors of 'Good Grief'
No sooner had we been widowed than the advice came flooding in. Move, people urged us. Move house. Move on.

Now, both of us are extraordinarily lucky—depending on your definition of the word. Mother and daughter, we enjoyed the extraordinary luck of loving and being loved for many years by wonderful men, John and Andy. When they died, just forty-one days apart, we perfectly understood what the other was going through, our grief for our husbands comingling with anguish at the loss of a beloved son-in-law, a cherished stepfather.

Our luck held in other ways too. Yes, the first lockdown came hard on the heels of our joint bereavements, but at least we had been able to sit with John and Andy, stroke their beautiful faces as they lay dying. At least we were able to hold commemorations for them. So many who lost loved ones in the pandemic were denied these things.

And somehow, in the depths of our grief, we knew to resist all that well-meaning advice about moving on. It helped that we had each other, if at the physical distance Covid precautions enforced. But more than that, we were supported by John and Andy. Love doesn't die with those you love. It lives on and sustains.

The idea of grief as an obstacle course with defined stages – denial, anger, bargaining, depression, acceptance – is widespread. It can also be misguided, especially if the end goal and prize is assumed to be getting rid of grief, moving on. For us, as for many others among the bereaved, the better ambition is to embrace grief, as you embrace those you love.

For our lovely dead do not leave us. Every day is full of memories and the joy those memories bring. One of us writes letters to her dead husband. The other holds daily conversations with hers. They are in every corner of our homes, in music and images that catch us unawares, in places we visited together.

This isn't denial, or the madness of grief. Each of us is living life to the full among the living. Our lovely dead are not barriers to this process but intrinsic to it, a huge part of our lives now and always. We are who we are because we love and were loved.

Grief is love, its price, but also its reward.
© *Anne Mayer Bird and Catherine Mayer*

Professor Olivette Otele
Distinguished Research Professor of The Legacies and Memory of Slavery at SOAS, University of London.
Trust in your ability to work harder. Trust in your vision and dreams.

Believe that you will always find a helping hand and incredible kindness on your journey through life.

Wake up hopeful and sleep thankful no matter what happens during the day.

David Peace
Writer

In my fifty-six very odd years here, I've been very fortunate to have heard or read many words that have helped me in both bad times and good, from family and friends, from football managers and saints, and football managers who were saints, from both Jesus Christ and Karl Marx, and most of all from novels and from poems but all of which, in many ways, can be distilled to the final lines of *The Mower* by Philip Larkin which suggest:

"we should be careful
Of each other, we should be kind
While there is still time."

Dr Alastair Santhouse
Psychiatrist

There's something about being a psychiatrist that lets you see the world in a different way.

I sit down every day and hear people talk about the most difficult and challenging times of their lives. They usually find it difficult to cope and I often feel immense sympathy for their suffering. However, as I listen to them talk about their most intimate feelings, I realise that there is a realm in which I am nearly powerless. What people experience in their lives is often beyond my control and something that psychiatric treatment cannot easily change.

Recently, I found myself back in my childhood home in the leafy suburbs of Manchester. The passing of time there felt more acute as I sat down next to my father who had just suffered a stroke. Like my patients, I felt at the whim of the unfeeling universe, finding it difficult to reckon with the effect of the stroke on my father and the sadness it was causing me and my family.

I prescribed myself a visit to Synagogue on the Saturday morning, where my father had been going for years.

Expecting to find spiritual guidance from within religious confines, it was strangely a conversation with the security guard that I went away thinking about. He asked me why I was visiting and I told him everything that had been going on in recent weeks. He seemed to recognise my anxiety and feelings of helplessness, but balanced it with a sense of caring optimism: "It's difficult," he concluded, "but love is above everything."

It sounded like the sort of phrase that must have existed forever, but it was the first time I had heard it put this way, and it stopped me for a moment.

We can all benefit from love. It is the glue that binds us together and supports us in the most difficult moments. Years of listening to people talk about their lives made me realise that we all seek human connection and a desire to experience the love that transcends whatever adversities life hands us; that love can make difficult times more bearable, it can make calculated risks worth taking, and it limits how far you can fall.

Wisdom can come from anywhere and at the most unexpected moments. And love is above everything.

Yvette Williams MBE
Justice 4 Grenfell Campaigner

In 1997 my dad died suddenly. He was my hero.

He passed when my sister was in hospital seriously ill, I had just left an acrimonious relationship and I needed to get out of a toxic workplace. I was at my lowest and devastated, but had to be strong for my mum and family who were relying on me to get things done.

At the funeral my cousin from the USA hugged me, gave me a book, and said, "Read it when you're ready, you will heal".

I thought it odd at the time and put it down to a bizarre American custom she had picked up. Suffering insomnia for days, I opened the book to fill my time. I read the first page and the tears began to fall. I realised that I hadn't cried since my dad had left us. I couldn't stop the tears from falling. What I read changed my life.

The book was by African American author Iyanla Vanzant. It is titled *The Value in the Valley*. I still go to my battered copy every so often.

Why?

It taught me that it is often at the lowest points in our life, those times when we believe it cannot get any worse; when we cannot see where we are going or understand why bad things happen; when you are in "the Valleys", is often the time where we learn the greatest lessons and trust what our purpose is in life.

The book offers no miracles and no guarantees that you will not face sad, difficult or devastating times. It taught me to find ways out of those times by drawing on my inner thoughts and resources and identifying the things only I could change.

I likened it to an iceberg – you watch it bashed by huge waves that erode its surface, but often the interior keeps rebuilding itself. My biggest "valley" challenge was learning not to absorb others' wounds and fractures but rather to push my energy out to them.

I've also learnt to be honest when I just need time out.

But the greatest gift the book gave me was permission to cry. Not only is it healing in the valley, but on your climb out there are tears of joy and laughter too.

Chrissie Wellington OBE
Triathlete and Ironman World Champion (4 x Ironman Triathlon World Championships, 1 x ITU Long distance World Championships and 1 x ITU Age Group World Championships)

I see my life as a tree, branching out in who knows what directions.

There is never a destination, just the impulse to grow. My only policy throughout has been to keep an open mind and, whatever I may do, to give it my all. It still takes my breath away to think of where that simple outlook on life has taken me, how many times I have managed to defy what I thought possible. I never set out to be world champion – not many ordinary girls from Norfolk do – but neither have I ever wanted to be left wondering, "What if…?"

To my amazement, at so many stages along the way, the limits that I thought I could see in the distance dissolved as I approached

them. They turned out not to be real at all, but mere assumptions. And that has been the most exciting revelation of all.
(From *A Life Without Limits: A World Champion's Journey*, Chrissie Wellington)

Dan Snow MBE
Historian and Televison Presenter
Stay curious.

The happiest people I've met have been the most curious.

The likelihood of your existence is infinitesimally small. The universe is endlessly fascinating. Your brain is the most sophisticated object in the observable universe. Cherish it, use it, stretch it, challenge and surprise it.

Revel in your existence... we're not here for long.

Dennis Reed
Director, Silver Voices
I was inspired to set up Silver Voices eight years ago by watching a series of discussions on TV on older people's issues, including pensions, ageism and social care.

Why is it, I thought, that UK society feels it acceptable for older people's rights and challenges to be discussed without the voices of older people themselves being expressed?

The normal pattern is for a video package to be shown, generally portraying older people as victims, followed by a studio discussion about the solutions, conducted with young academics or charity workers. Silver Voices is redressing this imbalance and fighting age discrimination wherever it occurs.

Vanessa Kirby
Actor
One of the best pieces of advice I ever received was, "Take care of your insides, and the outsides will take care of themselves" – look to change things inwards, before seeking to only change things on the external.

Or a long-winded version would be to go inwards, into self-reflection and enquiry, get to know all parts of yourself with compassion and self-forgiveness and the external things in life will follow, not the other way round.

Another one was, "Be present to what is in conversation with all that is".

Brian Cox CBE
Actor
My mother told me when I was a wee boy, "What's for you will not go by you".

Dickie Bird OBE
Former England Cricket Umpire
I always listened to my father's words. He was a true Christian, and he said, "No late nights, no nightclubs, no drinking if you want to get to the top."

Oliver Burkeman
Writer and Journalist
I find it deeply helpful to remember just how tiny – completely insignificant, really – any individual human life is, when set against the vast sweep of cosmic time.

I see why some people would find that depressing, or why it might cause them to wonder if there's any point in doing anything. But I find it freeing and life-enriching, because it's a reminder that our actions need not "matter" in some grandiose sense in order to matter in a more down-to-earth, human way. It stops me getting stuck in "analysis paralysis" or all twisted up about whether a given decision is the right one.

The fact that most or all of what I do today won't matter in a hundred years is a reason to make the bold career move; to reach out to the friend you've fallen out of touch with; to book the overseas trip; to make the kind gesture.

Now is when things count.

> **Righty tighty lefty loosey!**

Sara Cox
Broadcaster

Roger Kirby
President of the Royal Society of Medicine, Co-founder and President of the Charity The Urology Foundation (TUF), Vice-president of the Charity Prostate Cancer UK and Former Urological Surgeon

I have two pithy maxims that I often pass on to my patients and friends:
1. "Keep a steady nerve" – if you stayed chilled things have a way of working out fine over time.
2. "Roll with the punches" – life deals everyone some bad cards from time to time – but if you relax and take the hits – the sun eventually starts to shine again and the bruises disappear.

Dr Max Pemberton
Full-time Psychiatrist in the National Health Service, Newspaper Columnist and Editor

That man has just spat at me. It takes a while for what has happened to sink in. He definitely spat at me. I'm not sure what to do. No one has ever spat at me before. No one's coming to my rescue because I'm not on a ward, and the person who's just spat at me isn't a patient. He's just a random passer-by. I hadn't even looked at him, let alone actually done something to provoke such an attack.

I turn to the man sitting next to me. "Don't worry" he says, "they're always doing that sort of thing".

I stare at him and he takes a slurp of soup from the polystyrene cup, undeterred.

I'll be honest with you that when I took a job working with homeless people, I was a little scared. I have to try and engage with some pretty mean and nasty people. I knew it was going to be tough at times but I never thought I'd be on the receiving end of this. The man sitting next to me isn't outraged because he's used to it.

As I sit there it dawns on me that the man who had spat at me had done so because he thought I was someone else. He didn't realise that I was a doctor, sitting down on the pavement trying to persuade a patient with a gangrenous leg that he should come with me to the hospital. The brutal truth is that he spat at me because he thought I was homeless too. And so for a brief moment I learnt what it was like to be on the lowest rung of the social pecking-order, quite literally scratching around in the gutter to survive. I was on the receiving end of what the homeless people I work with experience on a daily basis.

"I got a kicking at the weekend," said the homeless man sitting next to me. "They're always doing it. I'm an easy target, what with my leg."

I look down at his leg, which technically is dead from the knee down and beginning to rot. It smells appalling.

"Sometimes they spit, sometimes they just shout at you. Other times it gets nasty and they try and duff you up," he explains, while continuing to drink his soup.

It would be easy to blame this sort of thing on louts and thugs; the disaffected youth. But the man who spat at me was wearing a tie. Perhaps it shows that one really can't judge a book by its cover: while he'd mistaken me for a homeless person because I was sitting on the pavement, I assumed because he looked presentable and was well dressed that he was a decent bloke.

The man next to me agrees to come into hospital and so I try and help him stand. I struggle. A boy standing over the road is watching, and after a few minutes he saunters over. He's wearing a baseball cap and hoodie and for a moment my heart sinks. I'm really not in the mood for any more trouble. But as he gets nearer he calls out, "You wanna hand?"

Together we help the homeless man to stand, and together we support him until the ambulance arrives.

Gary Davies
DJ

When I was trying to get a job in radio I spent two years making demo tapes which I sent to every radio station in the country, only to be rejected by all of them, time after time.

I was driving with my late dad, Gordon, and he asked me how it was going. I replied, "You know I've been trying for such a long time and nobody is interested. I think I'm going to give up."

I was expecting a sympathetic response along the lines of, "Don't worry son, it's tough out there but at least you've tried".

But that was exactly what I didn't get. He simply said, "Clearly you don't want it enough".

At the time I was so upset by his reaction and lack of sympathy, but when I thought about it he was absolutely right. As soon as I dropped him off at home I went and made yet another demo tape, and that was the one that got me my first job in radio.

Dad taught me an important lesson. If you really want something in life, you will never get it by quitting.

Rhian Mannings MBE
CEO and Founder 2Wish and Pride of Britain Award Winner

I was lucky growing up. I had wonderful parents who gave my sister, Sian, and I so many opportunities. I loved school, went off to university and got the first job I applied for after completing my PGCE. I loved life, faced everything with a positive attitude and tackled everything head on. There were few bumps in the road and I was blessed to be surrounded by so much love.

After meeting my husband, Paul, on a blind date, we married eight years later and had three amazing children in three years.

And that's where life as I knew it ended.

On 22nd February 2012 our youngest son, George, died.

No sign of illness and no warning, gone forever.

How do you come to terms with that?

Smiling and giggling and two hours later, gone.

With no support there for us, we relied on each other, family and friends to put one foot in front of the other. We told Holly and Isaac that George would shine like a star for all to see and muddled through our shock and grief. We would be OK, we reassured each other. We can do this, whatever this would become.

Five days later, what little of my life I had left, came crashing down. Paul, my husband, best friend and rock walked out of the house and took his own life.

I had no idea how we, as a family of three, could or would, recover. The light had gone out in my life, and I never thought we would come out of the darkness.

However, darkness is temporary.

The morning has to come and at night, the sky is lit with stars. Every night the children and I would look at the stars, looking for the brightest two. We were all consumed in sadness and grief but the sprinkling of stars inspired us to keep going. Similarly, in the rain we look for the rainbows, especially double ones. Despite the weather, there is always light.

From the moment I lost the boys, I was determined to grab hope by the hand and never let go. Hope has guided me through the darkest times. I had the children who were my stars in the darkness and the rainbows in the rain. There is always a positive. It may take years of pain to find it but never give up.

Keep looking up.

Laurence Halsted
Olympic Fencer and Author (European Championship Silver Medallist and 3 x European Championship Bronze Medals)
I was one of those athletes who took losing to heart.

As a kid I would be in floods of tears after being knocked out of youth tournaments, feeling down for days or sometimes even weeks after the event. The final time I cried after a defeat I was aged twenty-four and competing in a World Cup, the highest standard of tournament below the World Championships and Olympics.

At the time I believed that I *should* feel awful when I lost, as that would give me the motivation to work harder and do better next time. But the emotional backlash from losing was so bad that I would start to feel the anxiety of it during my fights. It weighed on me, distracting me from my performance, clouding my focus and making the whole thing incredibly stressful.

Then, during a period of injury in the run-up to the 2012 Olympic Games in London, I started working with a wonderful sport psychologist who helped me realise that if I was doing my best in performance then it simply didn't make sense to beat myself up if I made a mistake or lost a match – that's just part of sport.

It was a simple message but it felt like a revelation for me.

I started focussing far more on the process and less on the result, and I became much kinder and more forgiving to myself when things didn't go my way.

We tend to think of athletes as having incredibly high standards, never accepting anything less than perfect, so it might seem counter intuitive that an elite athlete should be kind to themselves when things go badly. But I suddenly found that I could focus far better, and I wasn't being plagued by anxiety the minute things got tough. I was able to perform with far more joy and freedom than ever before. My results got better and more consistent than ever before, and I was enjoying the entire process. I began to see the power of a self-compassionate approach.

At the Rio de Janeiro Olympics in 2016, during my debut in the individual event, on the biggest stage and under the glaring spotlights, I got off to a disastrous start – within three minutes, I was 8-1 down to my Chinese opponent in a match to fifteen points. My younger self would have been flooded by fear and anxiety at the prospect of a humiliating loss. However, my new, more compassionate perspective meant that I could maintain a calm, yet fierce, determination to fight my way back into the match. I didn't win that match, but I came right back in it, and it is one of the performances I am most proud of.

In sport we are great at being generous, kind and supportive to our teammates, but far worse at playing that role for ourselves. But it doesn't make any sense to treat ourselves worse than others we care about.

The true power lies not in self-criticism but in self-compassion.

Henry Dimbleby MBE
Entrepreneur and Writer
Stuff leads to stuff.

Christopher Timothy
Actor
The valued thrive.

Christopher Biggins
Actor

I am constantly asked by young actors for advice on the business called showbusiness and my reply to all of them is: Don't do it.

Now this may seem harsh, but I always qualify this by saying it's a tough business and nothing to do with talent, but always about being in the right place at the right time.

I know thousands of actors who are brilliant but never get the break.

One day they might get the break. It's nothing to do with age. A great friend of mine, Peggy Mount, was sixty when she became a star – so never give up.

However have a second string to your bow. I know this sounds harsh but one day you'll thank me for earning a penny or two to keep off the streets.

Ben Soames
Director, Fox Delta and Royal Marine

Train hard, fight easy.

The Royal Marines Commando course is the culmination of many months of grinding training, where recruits are continually challenged to find and then exceed their physical and mental limit. The experience is expansive, but deeply painful.

A common debate pervading the accommodation blocks in training centres is its relevance in elite military training. Does it need to be so hard, and is it still relevant for today's net-centric warfare?

I remember remarking to myself after emerging from the famous "sheep dip" on the endurance course element of the test, that it's not just a case of, "I don't know how I am going to pass this," but, "I don't know how anyone passes it."

A mantra used to program recruits by the training team whilst subjecting us to some new privation was, "Train hard, fight easy", as though this statement made it all make sense. At the time, it didn't, and usually drew an eye roll from the lads.

But something happens when you get through.

By graduation, the mental control that you have developed through the hardship is hard-wired into one's system. Every endeavour, from that moment, will be approached with total focus and commitment. Preparation and planning represents the larger portion of the mission, to the point where its execution becomes muscle memory.

Whilst the oft quoted phrase, "No plan survives contact with the enemy", still holds, I've learned that training hard, exceeding your limits prior to the engagement, will always result in more optimal outcomes.

Recently, I've taken to offering similar advice to my kids as they battle through exams. Remarkably, they seem completely unconvinced!

David Brabham
Professional Racing Driver
One bit of advice was racing related: when racing in Go Karts at 17 I was told "if you want to go quicker, less brake and more throttle". That didn't always work!

One bit of advice I tell my children is, "if you want a glimpse of your future, just take a look at yourself in the mirror. Who and what are you being right now in this moment and this will be your future, if you don't like it, change your thinking to create a new you and this will create a new future."

Ashley Scott
Paramedic
Calm in the chaos.

On many occasions as a paramedic I have attended incidents that appear stressful and sometimes chaotic. For the patients and their families, it is often a time of worry, pain and fear, possibly the worst day of their lives. For a medical first responder it can be a time of challenge.

In such situations there is an expectation that you will have all the answers, that you will make a difference and take away the worry, ease the pain and dispel the fear.

When all eyes fall on you, and you see that expectation, it can be daunting. So, take a breath, a deep one. Take those brief few seconds to create a calm in the chaos, focus your thoughts, accept the challenge and do your best to meet that expectation.

We cannot guarantee the outcome of any incident we attend, but we can always make a difference.

The calm we can bring to the chaos can be that difference, and a pause for a breath can make that possible.

Andy Airey
3 Dads Walking

The day we learnt that our beautiful daughter, Sophie, had taken her own life we had a visit from our vicar, Stewart. He said, "Some people will tell you that time is a great healer. That's rubbish.

"You'll always have a Sophie-shaped hole in your lives. That can never be filled in. At the moment, all you can see is that gaping void. As time goes by you will begin to find and do things that slowly start to insulate you from the hole. It won't go away but you won't fall in as often as you will over the next few weeks."

Four years after losing Sophie I know how right Stewart was.

Grief doesn't go away, it's always there.

We do have a Sophie-shaped hole in our lives that can never be filled but life does go on (whether you like it or not). In these four years we have changed, we have found things that slowly build protection around that hole. It's still there. We occasionally fall in but not as often as we used to.

The pain you suffer is a reflection of the love you have for the person you miss.

Don't be hard on yourself, feeling terrible about your loss is OK, it's normal, but remember to go on living your own life. It's the only one you've got.

Tim Owen
3 Dads Walking

When my daughter, Em, who was just nineteen, took her own life at the start of the pandemic there are no words to describe how I felt.

Devastated, destroyed, crushed, heart-broken do not even come close.

Just living took up all my strength and I did not know how to exist. I did not know where to turn or what to do. I was totally lost.

I remembered a speech by Admiral William McRaven of the US Navy about his ten principles for getting through life. For some reason his words had struck home to me and came back in that horrendous aftermath.

His opening principle was simply, "Make your bed".

His reasoning?

It is those small steps which matter. If you get up and the first thing you do that day, and possibly the only thing you do that day, is to make your bed then you will have achieved something positive. If you do nothing else all day, when you go to bed later you will be able to look at that bed and think that you achieved something; that simple small task of making your bed. It is a first step.

In those first days after I lost Em, without knowing what else to do and how to survive, I always took that first step of the day and made my bed. It was a positive start to every day.

Mike Palmer
3 Dads Walking

Some of the most powerful stories we hear on our walks are from those who had once fallen into despair and in some cases attempted suicide. Yet now they are living the lives they want to. Maybe not every day is perfect, but they now feel the love and fulfilment that gives them a reason to live.

Is this not hope?

Tony Mowbray
Football Manager

If you want to connect with your team; if you want them to run through brick walls for you, you must expose your soul both in success and failure, in words and in actions.

Professor Sir Michael Marmont
Professor of Epidemiology and Public Health, University College London and Director of The UCL Institute of Health Equity.
The health of society tells us a great deal about that society.

Inequalities in health reflect inequalities in society. Improving health and reducing inequalities means improving society.

What more important goal could there be?

Zoe Sugg (Zoella)
Media Entrepreneur
My therapist told me something years ago that I still keep in my back pocket to this day. It really helped me and has also helped others when they've needed it.

I'm someone who struggles a lot with caring far too much about how others perceive me, or what they think of me, and with being a serious over-thinker in social situations both in real life and online. This was exasperating when my career boomed in online content creation and I was faced with millions of opinions of me every day (most were lovely, some were humorous, some were outrageous and some were really wrong).

We can all get bogged down with others' opinions of us, whether they're strangers on the internet or someone we've met in person.

My therapist said that all the time I spent worrying what others thought, or what they were saying about me, I was metaphorically letting them into my house to sit on my sofa. I was allowing them in, offering them a cuppa and giving them my time, in my living room, and cracking open my favourite biscuits.

The thing is, they weren't my people, I didn't invite them, they showed up banging on the door and I opened it.

We might not have control over what others think about us, or what they say about us, but we do have control over how much power we give those people over our feelings.

We can ignore them when they bang on the door because they don't always deserve to come into your home, your sanctuary, your safe space, and the only person allowing that, is you.

The Lord Foster of Thames Bank
Architect and Designer
Stay a student.

Professor John Paul Leach
Neurologist and Academic
As I sit looking at the blank page, I am tempted to start writing now and not stop to get the job done. If I can put something on paper and leave the job behind me then I can relax, having ticked another thing off the "To Do" list.

Of course I have a "To Do" list. I retired yesterday, and I've been getting through it well. It's been a long day. It's been a long thirty-seven years.

As a student I remember my first casualty department visit. After what seemed like ten minutes' work, I was taken into the staff tea room. While patients were waiting, we were eating toast and chatting. I was shocked that it was possible for the doctors and nurses to concentrate on something other than getting through the backlog.

Three years later, on entering a new ward as the junior doctor, I was handed a pile of case notes – all those who were coming in for operations next day. Two hours and six patients later, around a third of the way through, a nurse popped through the curtains and asked to speak for a minute. She knew best. With wisdom and kindness the team had provided tea and toast. I bolted the lot down, eager to go back and finish the list.

On day one of my retirement I see what went wrong.

For the guts of four decades I have been trying to get work finished so that I could have a stress-free break. Lunch breaks disappeared years ago; I took fewer holidays than I was due, added patients into clinics to guarantee that they would over-run, and spent more nights sitting at a laptop than I would care to admit.

The truth is that especially in the modern age, there will always be more work to be done, always more patients waiting to be seen, always more jobs around the house, always more shopping, more relatives to visit, deliveries to make.

The job is never done.

If I could go back to the younger me, tap him on the shoulder and give him some advice I would tell him to take the breaks as the opportunity arises. The benefits are clear – this is where work can be rethought and reframed, the tank refilled, energy regrouped, morale recovered. In a strange reversal of what the younger me thought, breaks are to be embraced and tolerated and the work is to be enjoyed.

It only took me thirty-seven years to learn it.

Take the break. Fill the tank. The work will still be there when you come back refreshed and ready to do it properly.

Jemima Olchawski
CEO The Fawcett Society

It's not you, it's the system.

In a world designed for men, by men, we must remember that, as women, we are often made to feel it is us that are wrong. But we need to question the system and ask if it is the system that needs fixing, not us.

Sir Rodric Braithwaite
Diplomat and Writer

In the end, people are all we have.

The greatest gifts are friends, family and a long-term companion with whom to share passion, love and ideas, and solve the worst problems life throws at us. But people also spend much of their time killing one another in large numbers. You have to keep reminding yourself that evil and ugliness are offset by natural beauty and human creativity, kindliness, good cheer and self-sacrifice.

The people I admire most are those who work long hours caring for others, and all those men and women worldwide who have to work and survive in conditions far worse than ours. I try hard not to feel superior to those who prefer power, prestige, money, or celebrity.

We all lose people who are close to us. Many of us do shameful things. Grief and guilt press in as one gets older. Then comes oblivion. We'll never know where our grandchildren will end up, what happens to Ukraine, or how many more times Boris will become Prime Minister.

Dr Paul Baylis
Consultant in Emergency Medicine, Northern Ireland
It's called "practise" for a reason.

I've been practising emergency medicine for over thirty years and have been privileged to experience a real Boys' Own career.

Highlights include being a first-hand witness to the last twitches of the bitter convulsions that were The Troubles in Northern Ireland; a tour of duty with the Navy; six months as a flying trauma doc with HEMS London; postings at Liverpool's Alder Hey Hospital and the Trauma Unit of Cape Town's Groote Schuur Hospital; plus I ran away to Oz a couple of times to recharge for a year, when I felt the scorch of NHS burnout.

It's been a rollercoaster ride with some amazing highs, but the nugget I'd like to share is how I've coped with the corresponding lows.

The truth is that no doctor gets every decision right every time, except Gregory House MD (and he's fictitious). The greatest challenge is learning how to manage in the wake of the handful of calls that you will get wrong.

I can console myself that I have always made my decisions with my patient's best interests at the forefront of my mind, and that I've always been quick to apologise and explain if I may have made a mistake. But still, when a patient has come to harm there is no escaping the court of your own shaving mirror and doctors carry such patients with them, and they think of them often.

Over the years I've boiled down my ruminations on this issue to a simple soothing phrase – it's called "practise" for a reason. We all know doctors "practise" medicine. But why, since the days of Hippocrates, has the medical profession surrounded itself with that particular word?

It's because it was always so.

Even good doctors occasionally make bad calls and when we

have erred we have a simple choice, either give up our calling, or accept that we "practise" medicine. We should constantly get better at it, and we have a responsibility to learn from our mistakes and carry on, but emerge from these experiences wiser.

I make fewer mistakes these days, but this is mainly because I'm now in charge of my emergency department and consequently I'm more often driving a desk than a resuscitation. I do still frequently dust off this nugget of wisdom, but these days it's usually to offer it as some solace when I'm counselling younger colleagues who have slipped up.

Maybe we should all give ourselves licence to "practise" life, and when we slip up, as we surely will, once we have taken responsibility for our decisions and learned from our mistakes, we should strive to be kind to ourselves, stop beating ourselves up and instead move on, but do so wiser for the experience.

Sir Antony Beevor
British Military Historian

The reason why social media has become such a snake pit of polarised and toxic opinions is because intellectual honesty is the first casualty of moral outrage.

Jeremy Vine
Broadcaster and Journalist

Don't be hard on yourself.

You aren't perfect and you shouldn't expect yourself to be. You've made mistakes; everyone does. You've said the wrong thing, you've done the wrong thing — there's no person in the world who hasn't. Love yourself. All your mistakes and regrets amount to nothing. In fact they made you who you are.

When it really, really goes wrong listen to Buddy Holly sing *True Love Ways* and reflect that this brilliant genius got on a plane that crashed, losing his life at 22.

I figure that every day we live beyond Buddy Holly is more than we had any right to.

John Motson OBE
Football Commentator
It is from Marcus Aurelius: "Always bear this in mind, that very little indeed is necessary for living a happy life."

Jane Garvey
Radio Presenter
I wish it hadn't taken me so long to realise that everyone has a story.

I still have my teenage diaries, and they are certainly a source of entertainment, but they also really embarrass me. I was so utterly self-involved, so devoted to navel-gazing, that I missed so much. How I wish that I'd asked more questions of the people around me. My own grandmother lived with us; she was born in 1900. We did talk. But not enough. I should have asked her a thousand questions a day about what she'd seen and what she'd lived through. But I was too busy and too important.

Or so I thought.

Russ Abbot
Musician, Comedian and Actor
Believe in what you wish to achieve. There will be detours and knockbacks along the way. But have patience, have faith, work hard towards your goals.

Above all, believe in yourself.

Dr Ben Reynolds
Consultant Paediatric Nephrologist, Glasgow
"Hope is not a strategy" – one for clinicians and patients, it's fine (and necessary!) to have hope for a good outcome or a solution, but rarely does hope alone get you there.

"The only person who truly has your best interests at heart is you" – this is a piece of career advice I was given and is 100% true. Everyone providing advice support may want the best for you but only ever in the context of what will also be best for them/ their service.

"The worst possible outcome is that you leave today the same as you were this morning" – for students stressing about exams/assessments and the hype has got too much for their mental health, important to remember that most of these things are about progressing in something and that failing usually means the status quo is maintained.

"If you're in danger/physically threatened, shout FIRE" – one that I give at my women's self defence classes. Human nature is strange – if you shout help or rape, most people will walk past or hurry away. If you shout fire, most people will come to see what is happening. (You did say they could be very broad nuggets!)

A slightly wafflier one to finish, and harder for me to encapsulate in a sentence. Many many of our small children with significant CKD need supplemental feeding through a nasogastric tube or gastrostomy. It's so common that the vast majority will require this, and it is the minority that manage on oral feeds alone. I always stress to parents at the beginning that needing a tube does not mean that there has been any kind of failure by them/the child – as that is the expected outcome, but the unfortunate phrasing of "test of oral feeding" often implies that this is something you can pass/fail.

Sir Cameron Mackintosh
Theatrical Producer
In any walk of life, if you're starting out, try and make yourself indispensable. Do something that you feel passionately about. I never went into the theatre to make money; I just wanted to make successful shows so I could continue doing what I love.

Jo Brand
Comedian, Writer, Presenter and Actor
One of my mum's favourite quotes, from the obituary of the actor Frank Singuineau: "He had been an only child, raised by his mother and two aunts after his father's early death. In a recent interview he said, 'All the things I learnt I learnt from women. I realised from a very early age that I was very lucky in growing up in

the presence of a superior, smarter, stronger race. I had a different vision of what life should be'."

Alison Weir
Writer and Public Historian
An inspiring quote from the fourteenth century anchoress, Julian of Norwich, which has been a mainstay for me through life's tragedies and trials: "He said not, 'Thou shalt not be tempested, thou shalt not be travailed, thou shalt not be dis-eased'; but he said, 'Thou shalt not be overcome'."

Robert Rinder MBE
Criminal Barrister and Television Personality
Who are your real friends?

I've always known that true friends are the key to happiness.

That doesn't mean the ones who are just there for the hard times (there's a toxic type who are only there when times are tough. They love to crowbar themselves into the drama). No, the best and finest ones are those you can call when things are actually going well.

They don't die a little when you succeed, they're genuinely chuffed to bits.

When I received a bit of excellent news, a friend who knew exactly how good it was immediately got on the blower to congratulate me. He had no reservations about telling me how thrilled he was ... and it filled me with the purest kind of gladness. It said everything that was relevant and necessary about this wonderful person, because the best friends are there through thick and thin, for better just as much as for worse (and – what's more – they'll know you better than any computer algorithm).

If you find some, never let them go.

The Lord Kestenbaum
Chief Operating Officer of Investment Trust RIT Capital Partners plc.
"Stay close to those who speak to the better angels of our nature, and thereby get the best out of us".

Professor Sallie Baxendale
Professor of Clinical Neuropsychology, University College London
"It takes a great deal of bravery to stand up to your enemies, but a great deal more to stand up to your friends"

This is a quote from the movie adaptation of *Harry Potter and the Philosopher's Stone*. Albus Dumbledore, the wise old Headmaster of Hogwarts proclaims this when awarding winning house points to class klutz Neville Longbottom, after he has taken a principled stand against his friends, Harry, Hermione and Ron. There are two versions of the quote. In the original book, Dumbledore says "It takes a great deal of bravery to stand up to our enemies, but just as much to stand up to our friends." In the movie he says a great deal more to stand up to your friends. I prefer the movie version. It is exceptionally hard to stand up to our friends when we think they have got something wrong, and all too easy to sit back, say nothing and keep our heads down. This doesn't get any easier as we get older. Much of the human misery in the world from the playground to the global stage can be viewed through this lens; a failure to find this very special kind of courage. This nugget is a reminder that if we want a better world we must all strive to be braver in this respect.

Mark Ormrod
Former Royal Marine, Athlete, Invictus Games,
Writer and Motivational Speaker
Failure isn't fatal and it isn't final if you learn from it and carry on trying.

You may not always hit your target first time but if you take the lessons from it, adjust accordingly and keep trying then eventually you'll get where you want to be.

We only develop a fear of failure as we get older and are more exposed to the world. When we're babies and we're learning to walk we constantly "fail" and we usually do it with a smile on our face and try again. Eventually even at such a young age we learn what we did right, what we did wrong and we're able to walk. Imagine if we gave up after the first couple of tries? We'd all look pretty silly as adults crawling everywhere because we were too scared to keep trying to learn how to walk.

So change your mindset, understand failure is part of the journey, embrace it, learn from it, grow from it and then use it to lead you to success.

John Volanthen
Cave Diver and Rescuer, South and Mid Wales Cave Rescue, and the British Caving Association
Start with, "Why not?"

The first steps are often the hardest. Too often we are guilty of giving up on an idea because the end goal feels overwhelming. Think positively, take action.

You are stronger and more capable than you imagine.

Dame Darcey Bussell
Ballerina and Former Strictly Come Dancing Judge
Carry a positive attitude into every day and in turn you will receive a positive outcome.

Sitting for too long will drain your energy. Movement and music always help create strength within you.

Hugh Dennis
Comedian, Presenter, Actor, Impressionist and Writer
Because north London provides limited opportunities for gold prospecting, and I find the idea of fried chicken in a bucket about as appetizing as slow-cooked anchovies in a washing-up bowl, my favourite kind of nuggets are an alternative type – nuggets of information. Not useful information mind you, because that wouldn't be quite as entertaining. No, my kind of nuggets are those small, and occasionally intriguing pieces of information contained in Tannoy announcements.

Although mindful of the fact that for most people the main part of the word "Tannoy" is "annoy" I have come to enjoy them and if I hear one that I particularly like, to note it down. Trains, on which I spend a great deal of time, are a particularly fertile area. In fact, it was while travelling on a South-West Train that my noting habit began. Well, I say travelling, we were in fact completely motionless, stuck tantalisingly close to Waterloo, and had been for about ten minutes, when the train manager delivered the following message: "We apologise for the wait outside Waterloo. This is due to a delay."

And to be fair to him he was right, because the two words mean precisely the same thing. Clearly, I would have preferred a useful piece of information to a tautology, but it was at that point, or more precisely at those points, that I began to make my collection. Only a few weeks later I was rewarded with an announcement on a GWR not as fast as it should be service to Bristol, made by a train manager clearly frustrated by a situation she faced almost every day. The start of the announcement was familiar, but the conclusion unexpected.

"We apologise for the wait outside Bath," she said. "This was due to two decades of chronic underinvestment in the railway industry."

Which seemed a fair appraisal of the situation. Others have followed from guards with a similar view of the world. En-route to Edinburgh: "For your information this train has one quiet carriage. The rest are so old and rattly, you can't hear yourself think."

On the way from London to Norwich: "Due to a points failure, the next station stop will be Edinburgh."

And three hours into a two-hour journey to Manchester: "Just to remind passengers there is a buffet trolley on this train. Just a trolley, nothing on it, not even a flap-jack".

My favourite however remains the platform announcement I heard when standing at Haywards Heath Station on my way to Gatwick. It was very simple: "Southern would like to apologise for the cancellation of all services … well I'll be … there's one coming!"

And I am certain there will be more to come. Given the state of the railways I am just willing a station announcer to say: "The train on Platform 12 is the delayed 19:57 from Guildford. So just sixty-six years late then."

> When I set off for work for the very first time, my dad said there were two essentials to find out as soon as possible: first, where the toilets are, and second how to fill in an expense claim form.

Sir Peter Wanless
CEO, NSPCC

Stephen Bate MBE
Cyclist (2 x Paralympic Champion, 3 x Road World Championships Champion, Track World Championships Champion, Paralympic Silver Medallist, 3 x Road Championships Silver Medals and Paralympic Bronze Medallist)

Staying mentally and physically present in the moment is the best way to maximise success. When things become overwhelming, our minds start to wander and our focus is lost. Normally this leads to those little voices of self-doubt creeping in. Take a deep breath, feel the connection to the ground by pressing your toes into your footwear, and bring your attention back to your current situation.

Focus on the process, not the outcome.

George Monbiot
Journalist and Author

It would be easy to curse my luck and start to ask, "Why me?"

I have never smoked and hardly drink; I have a ridiculously healthy diet and follow a severe fitness regime. I'm twenty or thirty years younger than most of the men I see in the waiting rooms. In other words, I would have had a lower risk of prostate cancer only if I had been female. And yet ... I am happy. In fact, I'm happier than I was before my diagnosis. How can this be?

There are three principles which, I believe, sit at the heart of a good life. The first is the most important: imagine how much worse it could be, rather than how much better. The tragedy of our times is that, rather than apply the most useful of English proverbs – "cheer up, it could be worse" – we are constantly induced to imagine how much better things could be. The rich lists and power lists with which the newspapers are filled, our wall-to-wall celebrity culture, the invidious billions spent on marketing and advertising, create an infrastructure of comparison that ensures we see ourselves as deprived of what others possess. It is a formula for misery.

The second principle is this: change what you can change, accept what you can't. This is not a formula for passivity (I've spent my working life trying to alter outcomes that might have seemed immovable to other people). But sometimes we have to accept an obstacle as insuperable. Fatalism in these circumstances is protective.

The third principle is this: do not let fear rule your life. Fear hems us in, stops us from thinking clearly and prevents us from either challenging oppression or engaging calmly with the impersonal fates. There are, I believe, three steps to overcoming fear: name it, normalise it, socialise it. For too long, cancer has been locked in the drawer labelled Things We Don't Talk About. When we call it the Big C, it becomes, as the term suggests, not smaller, but larger in our minds. He Who Must Not Be Named is diminished by being identified, and diminished further when he becomes a topic of daily conversation. There is evidence to suggest that a caring community enhances recovery and reduces mortality. In talking about my cancer with family and friends, I feel the love that I know will get me through this. The old strategy of suffering in silence could not have been more misguided. Let there be no more terrible secrets.
(From "Unprostrated", by George Monbiot,
The Guardian, 13th March 2018)

Dr Chris Van Tulleken
Doctor and Broadcaster

My nugget of wisdom is impossible to follow: Don't lie.

If you make this promise to yourself you'll start to notice your discomfort with even the little exaggerations and distortions of the truth that we all use to get through life. You should feel uneasy at these, and that unease should make you unable to tell a deliberate lie. Deliberate lies are little patches over our flaws and mistakes that allow those flaws to grow and the mistakes to multiply.

And they're addictive.

If you lie to some people you lie to everyone, including yourself, and these are the most dangerous type of lies.

Gyles Brandreth
Broadcaster and Writer

Theodore Roosevelt, President of the United States, gave his name to the teddy bear and also gave me one of my favourite nuggets of wisdom: "Do what you can, with what you have, where you are."

Dame Joanna Lumley
Actor, Presenter, Author and Television Producer
Salutation to the Dawn, based on a Vedic hymn:

> 'Look to this day
> For it is life:
> The very life of life.
> In its brief course lie all
> The realities and verities of existence:
> The bliss of growth,
> The splendour of action,
> The glory of power.
> For yesterday is but a dream,
> And tomorrow is only a vision;
> But today, well lived,
> Makes every yesterday a dream of happiness
> And every tomorrow a vision of hope.
> Look well, therefore, to this day.'

Stig Abell
Journalist, Newspaper Editor and Radio Presenter
The best piece of wisdom I ever read was by the screenwriter William Goldman: "Nobody knows anything".

He was talking about Hollywood, but it holds true for everywhere.

It is an antidote to imposter syndrome: you should never feel down upon yourself or your abilities or your prospects, because everybody is struggling, everybody is making it up as they go along.

I have interviewed the most powerful people in the country and can tell you that they don't know much; they are as fallible as the rest of us. So if everybody is flawed, why shouldn't you succeed; if somebody has to come out on top, why shouldn't it be you?

Nobody knows anything.

It's reassuring when you think about it.

Debbie McGee
Television, Radio and Stage Performer
My step grandson Lewis Daniels was diagnosed with kidney disease at university.

At first we all, including the doctors, thought it would be treatable for some years with medication. Unfortunately this was not to be the case. Lewis had a kidney transplant.

He is such an inspiration. Despite this changing the course of his career and his life, he has never complained and is always smiling. He deals with his condition on a daily basis. He has changed his career ambition and is now aiming for that.

During the pandemic he started a podcast talking to other transplant patients so they could share stories of how they were coping. He is twenty-two and I am so proud of him.

My nugget is: "Look to people who are coping in worse situations than you and try and find their strength."

Bonnie Langford
Actor, Dancer and Singer
The next time you're faced with something that's unexpected, unwanted and uncertain, consider that it just may be a gift.

Nick Knowles
Television Presenter, Writer and Musical Artist
When you feel like you are in tough times and can't see a way forward, deal with the next thing only, not the bigger picture.

Put one foot in front of the other and eventually you will find you have walked over the mountain you were facing.

Siobhán McSweeney
Actor and Presenter
"Never mind
It doesn't matter what you look like
All that matters is you dance
Cause it's a very very short life."
Dizraeli and the Small Gods.

Annette Badland
Actor
"Whatever you can do or dream you can, begin it.
Boldness has genius, power, and magic in it."
Attributed to the German playwright and thinker Goethe

"In ancient times cats were worshipped as gods;
they have not forgotten this."
Terry Pratchett.

"Be curious, not judgemental."
Walt Whitman
(but I first heard it from the character of Ted whilst filming *Ted Lasso*)

Debbie Wiseman OBE
Composer, Conductor and Presenter
If you love your work, you end up never doing a day's work in your life.

I love my job – working in music is a great privilege. If you can strive towards finding a job that you can immerse yourself in and find rewarding then work becomes play.

Even though my schedule can mean taking fewer holidays, and often not having weekends off, I don't mind the sacrifices. My working day is stimulating and enjoyable, the rewards so much higher.

The saying "work hard, play hard" doesn't mean much to me, as my work is also my play. If you can find a job that feels like play, then life is infinitely more enjoyable and rewarding.

Helen Lederer
Comedian, Writer and Actor
I have been inspired by the book *Feel the Fear and Do it Anyway* by Susan Jeffers.

I took a copy on my first UK tour as a stand-up comedian. It's about love. If I love the audience, it's OK.

"When we give from a place of love rather than from a place of expectation, more usually comes back to us than we could have ever imagined. Remember that underlying all our fears is a lack of trust in ourselves."

Cathy Courtney
Oral Historian and Writer
1. To help navigate the relationship between different eras of history, choose a figure from the past whose life you know about and memorise their birth and death dates. This will give you a peg on which to hang events in other centuries, whether distant or near to the period through which your chosen figure lived.

    A measuring post. For me, the figure is the architect and playwright John Vanbrugh, 1664-1726. Having a sense of the developments during Vanbrugh's lifetime helps situate other historical information in perspective to the world as it was for him.
2. I have been freelance all my working life. At the beginning I didn't have the confidence to believe I would succeed and I didn't take myself seriously enough to establish a filing system, let alone a filing system that would continue to make sense to me. So my advice to anyone starting out is to set up systems – whether digital or physical – right from the start and stick to them.
3. Sometimes people have to fight a long time to achieve a position in relation to work or another aspect of life. Once gained, it is important not to become its prisoner because it has been so difficult to reach. The ability to recognise when something has run its course is hard learnt.

Preferably take your leave as well as you can.

Eileen Hogan
Official Portrait Artist for the King and Queen's Coronation
My nugget came from someone I disliked a lot – a misogynist, sexist lecturer at Camberwell School of Art, when I was a student there in the 1960s.

"You will only do good work when you find out what you want to paint".

In order to be an artist, you really have to want to do it – long solitary hours, no guarantee of fame or even an income, so he was right.

The Lord Austin of Dudley
Politician, Life Peer in the House of Lords

My mum always used to say, "Do unto others as you would be done by," which I think is a pretty good rule to live by.

I have always thought you should be able to stand up to and tell people above you the truth, however uncomfortable it might be, but stand up for and be pleasant and polite to everyone else.

And finally, you should of course take your work and the difference you can make seriously, but never take yourself too seriously.

Oliver McTernan
Director, Forward Thinking

Always reach for the stars, no matter what your stars may be. It's only by thinking big and aiming high that we can reach our full potential. It is the fear of failure that stops most great ideas from flying, so think big and crazy and take those calculated risks.

Dr Maggie Aderin-Pocock MBE
Space Scientist, Science Educator and Broadcaster

When I was a student I was given a wise piece of advice by the late Bishop Christopher Butler.

"As your life develops", he told us, "you will receive many requests to attend meetings and to give talks. Never say 'yes' immediately. Take time to think of the consequence of agreeing. If the request comes by phone, ask them to put it in writing. If by letter take at least three days before responding."

In an age of instant communication it is certainly more difficult to follow such advice.

Looking back on my own life I wish I had been more disciplined in acting on this wise advice.

David Gower OBE
Former First-class English Cricketer and Commentator
I am happy to offer three stolen nuggets – I'm not clever enough to make up my own. All from *Older, Wiser Sexier*, collated by Bev Williams:

"You cannot turn back the clock. But you can wind it up again." (Bonnie Prudden)

"We learn from experience that men never learn from experience." (George Bernard Shaw)

"Good judgement comes from experience and often experience comes from bad judgement." (Rita Mae Brown).

Sir Derek Jacobi CBE and Malorie Blackman OBE
Actor and Writer
Sir Derek and Malorie selected the same quotation: "To thine own self be true, and it must follow as the night the day, thou can'st not then be false to any man." Polonius in *Hamlet*, by William Shakespeare.

Dr Kingsley Poole
GP, West Sussex
When I was 19 I lost my beloved younger brother, Sean.

For a few months I lived in a strange twilight zone where nothing felt real. For many years I quelled my soul through the sport of rowing, then later by writing novels and even a screenplay. In the thirty plus years since Sean died, I have essentially been transmuting my grief.

I picture grief as a millpond which continually fills with frustration, bitterness, anger and fear, and which will flood over if you let it. Or it can power the watermill, driving you forward and helping you realise your dreams.

The Rt Hon. Lady Justice Simler
Judge of the Court of Appeal of England and Wales
There is a saying of Churchill's that I reassure myself with and think is inspiring: "Success is not final, failure is not fatal: it is the courage to continue that counts".

Corrine Hutton
Finding your Feet Charity
After losing my hands and legs to sepsis (and nearly my life) I think I'm qualified to suggest that the human spirit is stronger than anything that can happen to it.

We all have the strength in us to get back up but we have to dig deep to find it. My kidneys are the latest failing in a long line of side effects but thankfully they are rebuilding me with used parts and I'm so grateful to the people brave and kind enough to want to give the gift of life.

I've got a second chance – I won't be wasting it!

John Inverdale
Broadcaster
Every minute spent in bed after the alarm has gone off is a minute you'll never get back. Get up.

Sharron Davies MBE
Swimmer (2 x Commonwealth Champion, 1 x Olympic Silver, 2 x Commonwealth Silver, 1 x Olympic Silver, 2 x Commonwealth Bronze and 2 x European Championship Bronze)
My dad, who was my coach and a driving force in my swimming years, used to re-tell this story at least once a week...

Supreme golfer Gary Player won his third US Open and a journalist offered his congratulations.

"Well done Gary, great play, you were lucky today," he said.

"Yes, funny that," Gary said, "the harder I train the luckier I get."

This story has always rung true for me, and though being in the right place at the right time is useful, luck is really where hard work meets opportunity.

I try to wish people multiple opportunities, and what they do with those is then up to them.

Maddy Warren
@queenofdialysis
Your medical condition doesn't define you.

It is part of you, but along with the challenges it also gives you strength, resilience and perspective. Harness those positives, use them to your advantage and believe in yourself. Remember not to listen to the uninvited opinions of people who you wouldn't choose to go to for advice.

Chief Rabbi Sir Ephraim Mirvis
Chief Rabbi of the United Hebrew Congregations of the Commonwealth
How should we respond to painful and traumatic experiences? Jewish tradition differentiates between fate and destiny. My fate is the hand of cards I'm dealt. My destiny is how I play that hand.

Whatever our circumstances, it is within the power of every one of us to carve out a glorious destiny for ourselves.

William Sieghart CBE
Entrepreneur, Publisher and Philanthropist
"I wish I could show you
When you are lonely or in darkness,
The astonishing light of your own being".
Hafez

Richard Pitman
*Jockey (2 x King George VI Chase Champion Hurdle,
Whitbread Gold Cup and Hennessy Gold Cup Winner)*
The thrill of riding in six Grand Nationals is something money cannot buy.

Three falls among the steel shod hoofs of the mass of half-ton horses were the lows. Two second places, including one on board Crisp, who was only caught in the final two strides by Red Rum, remain vivid in my memory.

Partnering top steeplechasers to win big races in front of huge crowds was such an exciting way to earn a crust.

However my decision to become a kidney donor in 2012 was the most satisfying thing I have ever done or could do.

My long-time friend Tim Gibson, who had received a kidney thirty-five years earlier, was experiencing life on dialysis and had become a wasted person in front of my eyes.

The stubborn, proud Yorkshireman was refusing to let me or his children test to see if we were able to give him a new kidney to extend his life. Tim was 8,003rd on the waiting list, which meant he was a long shot to find a match.

A young man who was fatally injured in an accident exactly matched Tim's kidney. I saw him go through this second operation to become the big strong man he had been, even resuming motor racing with the vigour of a man given a second bite of the cherry.

It occurred to me that I could do the same thing to help change someone's life, so began the extensive testing before donation.

Mind, body and the backing of my own family was needed before I was accepted to donate.

Amazingly my mind and body proved able, my wife and daughters backed me, so the journey began.

My kidney left my body and was working happily within hours within the unknown recipient. Within a week I was over the operation, three weeks later I was driving and just five weeks after I was back riding racehorses on the gallops. Only ten weeks after leaving hospital I rode in a veterans flat race at Aintree on Grand National day, miked up live for BBC TV. Within sixteen minutes of the finish I was interviewed and encouraged others to donate organs too.

My recipient and I shared letters. Despite having received many notes from winning owners and a handful of trophies, the first letter from my recipient made me weep tears of joy.

They wrote: "Having been on dialysis for seven years, I am now working my smallholding, you have given me my life back again."

That will remain with me forever.

Sir Stephen Hough CBE
Pianist, Composer and Writer
"For all that has been, Thanks; for all that will be, Yes."
Dag Hammarskjöld

Rhys James
Comedian, Writer and Television Presenter
Kidney nugget:
Even if you don't have any kidney issues, I recommend having one removed like I did, so you never have to play rugby in PE again.

Wisdom:
1 Young people, pick your greeting now. Are you a handshaker, a cheek-kisser, a hugger? Do you confidently back yourself to fist bump, regardless of the recipient? Choose your greeting and commit to it for the rest of your life. No more awkward hellos.
2 Success rarely feels like success, so try to birdseye-view it as much as possible and think what the you from a few years ago would think of how you're doing.
3 If you want to go jogging but don't want people to think you're the sort of loser who goes jogging, while you're doing it just point ahead and shout, "Stop that man!" Everyone will think you're chasing down a thief and laud you as a hero.
4 If your partner is spending a lot of time with your best friend, they're either having an affair, or they're secretly planning you a surprise party. You have to wait until your birthday to find out. If you're spending it alone, it's probably an affair. Or it's about to be an amazing surprise party.

Professor Sir John Cunningham
Professor of Renal Medicine
As far as possible make yourself easy to like and difficult to dislike.
    If someone likes you they will find it more difficult to raise the head of steam needed to give you a hard time.

> All this is chance, readiness is all.

Owen Teale
Actor

Professor Karim Brohi
Surgeon and Professor of Trauma Sciences,
Queen Mary, University of London

Be the climate, not the weather.

Climate is long term, persistent, consistent and expected. Weather is what happens today, which could be what you expected, or completely unexpected, good or bad, hurricane or heatwave. But all weather smooths out into climate.

"Be the climate" directs you to a more long-term view in all aspects of personal, home and work. Today's struggles become more manageable, as you know they will pass – indeed you can't remember those things that kept you up at night a year ago.

Think forwards for the long term, but also look back and see how far you've come. If you can be the steady force over long periods of time, then people know what you stand for, where you are headed, and they can grow and develop with you.

If winds block your progress today, know that all you need to do is still be there when the squall is past and you get the wind at your back again. And remember that climate is cyclical, seasons come and go, and come again.

Know when to hunker down for winters, and when to use energy for growth and transitions.

Be the climate, not the weather.

Also, don't go upstairs empty handed.

Helen Rogerson
Dialysis Patient

I live by a Bible quotation and a song quotation, which help me keep going during trials, especially the latest challenge going through cancer and now dialysis.

"I can do all things through him who strengthens me".
Philippians 4:13

"If I can help somebody as I pass along,
If I can cheer somebody with a word or a song,

If I can show somebody he is travelling wrong,
Then my living shall not be in vain".
Mahalia Jackson

Richard Dunwoody MBE
*Jockey (4 x King George VI Chase, 2 x Grand National,
Cheltenham Gold cup and The Champion Hurdle Winner)*
The only order that my first trainer, Captain Tim Forster, dryly gave to all his jockeys who rode for him in the Grand National was "Keep remounting." His version of "keep getting back on the horse". Despite his pessimism he trained three winners of the great race.

Pandora Sykes
Writer and Broadcaster
Everyone's life is entirely their own.

Your life might intersect with theirs on occasions (many occasions, if it's a best friend or family), but it's theirs and theirs alone. There's no point coveting what someone else has.

Follow your own path.

Alison Steadman OBE
Actor
My friend's mum died a couple of years ago at the age of 102.

I had known her since I was ten years old. She was a bright, energetic, positive woman. I can still see her smile. When she died her daughter found this quote she'd left: "Do not stain today's blue sky with tomorrow's clouds".

I love this and will carry it with me always.

The Hon. Mrs Justice Cheema-Grubb
Judge of the King's Bench Division of the High Court of Justice of England and Wales
Look at yourself, what you do, what you feel, with curiosity rather than judgment.

Cal Flyn
Writer and Journalist

As Picasso once said, "Inspiration does exist, but it has to find you working."

   I always find getting new projects off the ground very challenging; you are starting from nothing, and often only from a feeling or notion. Later, it will feel like the route was always obvious, that things simply fell into place, but not so – one has to move ahead blindly at first. But it's true that if you are actively looking for solutions, you'll tend to find them. Far less is achieved if you wait for solutions to come to you.

Jeremy Irons
Actor and Activist

"All men dream: but not equally.
Those who dream by night in the
dusty recesses of their minds wake
In the day to find that it was vanity.
But the dreamers of the day are
dangerous men, for they may act
their dreams with open eyes
to make it possible".
T.E. Lawrence

Debbie Chazen
Actor

Learn not to care what other people think of you.

   I find this easier the older I get, and when I was diagnosed with breast cancer in 2009 the realisation really hit home that our time on this big, beautiful, stupid, selfish, glorious planet is fleeting.

   We're all of us just trying to make it through each day without having a meltdown about work, or energy bills, or health, or love, or whether anyone's going to press the "like" button – or, some days, the "nuke" button. So do whatever it is that makes you happy, as long as you're not hurting anyone else.

Go swimming – everyone else is too busy worrying about what they look like in their swimsuit to worry about you.

Be creative – you don't have to be Picasso or Jimi Hendrix or Shakespeare to draw or noodle on an instrument or write a poem.

Join in the karaoke – sometimes the worst singers make for the best entertainers.

Stop comparing yourself to others – everyone else out there is just as scared and clueless as the rest of us.

Kim Leadbeater MBE
MP for Batley and Spen

There's never a good time to be ill, but even with the extreme pressure the NHS has been under, we can be thankful we live in a country where treatment is available free of charge.

Like most people, I have family and friends who have needed medical treatment, either in an emergency or to help deal with chronic illness. And we never know when we might be one of those people ourselves.

I have a background in health and fitness before becoming an MP, so I hope I'm pretty well aware of how the body works and how to keep it working well. But, if I'm honest, until recently I didn't give a lot of thought to my kidneys. We just don't, do we? They work away, twenty-four hours a day, without making any demands for our attention, and thank goodness they do.

I know now that kidney disease can range from the fairly mild to severe, and I was surprised to learn that as many as 16% of the adult population may have the markers of kidney disease.

A family member of mine needed a kidney transplant more than thirty years ago. She still has serious health issues but without that donor all those years ago she wouldn't be with us now. So I would encourage everybody to seriously consider organ donation because quite simply it saves lives. So too does taking up the offer of an NHS health check when you're eligible.

In 2021, just as I was making the move from community work through the Jo Cox Foundation into politics, my dad was diagnosed with kidney cancer following a routine blood test. I'm pleased to say that while the surgery took a lot out of him and the recovery has been slow and sometimes difficult, he's now doing really well.

Dad is well into his seventies but kidney cancer can strike at any age. Around the same time that dad got his diagnosis, my friend and colleague Wes Streeting, Labour's health spokesman, was told that he too had a tumour on his kidney. He was thirty-eight. Like Dad, he was operated upon successfully and fortunately the cancer hadn't spread.

We can't tell when illness, whether physical or mental, might strike and leave us in the capable hands of health professionals. What we can do is celebrate the fantastic work they do, under sometimes intolerable pressure, while doing everything possible to keep ourselves and our communities strong and healthy.

I'm a relentlessly positive person, but I also believe in talking about our problems as openly and constructively as possible.

I believe we're getting better at this, whether that's around cancer, mental illness or the many other challenges that come our way. That, too, is something to celebrate.

There's still a lot of work to be done, but also much to be thankful for. Together we can make a huge difference to the health and wellbeing of our country. It's not a task that will ever be marked "done" but I'm encouraged every day by the number of people who remain committed to doing what they can and who are determined never to give up.

Zeb Soanes
Radio Presenter

My father is a Methodist minister and his mentor, Rev. Norwyn Denny, passed on to him these wise words, "Always accept gifts graciously."

As I've gone through life I realise this applies to praise too. The very British trait of batting aside compliments is ungrateful, no matter how shy or self-critical you are. Just smile and say "thank you".

Professor Clare Finburgh Delijani
Professor of Theatre Studies, Goldsmiths, University of London

The best mentor I've ever had is Peter Hulme, who was a professor of postcolonial studies at the University of Essex when I first started working there. I sat in as he gave a PhD student feedback on her first chapter. She asked if she should write the chapter again to which he replied, "You could go on rewriting Chapter One forever. Or else you could start on Chapter Two."

This is now one of the most valuable pieces of advice I give my own students. Get it finished. Then you can go back and twiddle or tweak.

Simon Evans
Comedian and Broadcaster

I am a nugget magpie. I have a nestful of shiny epigrams, quotations and aperçus. I collect them, I snatch them up and I hoard them. I can quite easily imagine Kim and Aggie from that hoard-shaming show on the telly forcing open the door to one of the spare rooms in my brain and finding it stacked high with yellowing cuttings from long-forgotten magazines, on-line articles, overheard conversations and just occasionally, constructions of my own invention.

Quite how much these insights have helped guide me through life, and been reached for in a crisis, and how much they are mere adornments, flourished in conversation to demonstrate erudition and perhaps intimidate an opponent, is a good question. But there are one or two that have served me well, I think, and for these present purposes, I thought it might be worth sharing some that might stand out from the crowd.

GK Chesterton's warning, "Don't ever take a fence down until you know the reason it was put up", is perhaps the single most nuggety formulation of the conservative sentiments that I know, and was among the first to convince me that my more right-of-centre instincts, sometimes at odds with those of my drinking buddies, were not merely a pathology, and shameful in one so young.

Michael Oakeshott's illumination, "To be conservative … is to prefer the familiar to the unknown, to prefer the tried to the untried, fact to mystery, the actual to the possible, the limited to the unbounded, the near to the distant, the sufficient to the superabundant, the convenient to the perfect, present laughter to utopian bliss," is a little less nuggety perhaps – indeed, borders on the indulgent but is otherwise unsurpassed.

And finally, one of the first quotations I came across as an adult, in the preface to the *Hitch-Hiker's Guide to Europe*. It was from Gertrude Stein. She was actually referring to a specific neighbourhood, in Oakland, California, I believe. But it survives, because it is universal: "When you get there, there's no there there."

True.

Enjoy the ride

that's all there is.

Father Alex Frost
Vicar and Writer

I received an anxious call from a nursing home asking if I could visit one of my parishioners who was in the last stages of life. I jumped in my Citroen C3 and headed up.

Wendy was evidently approaching the final hours of her long and colourful life.

I had known for some time of Wendy's illness and so knew that when the time came, she would like me to anoint her with holy oils and administer the last rites. Wendy was in and out of consciousness, and as I explained what I would be doing, Wendy mustered enough strength to acknowledge that it was okay to proceed.

I carried out what I described, I anointed her with oil and recited the liturgy for such an occasion, and in Wendy's stillness I was melancholy with emotion. Once the rites had been administered I sat by Wendy's bed, held her hand and closed my eyes. Then Wendy whispered, "Thank you Father Alex. I want you to know that I'm going to pray for you now," and with that she fell asleep.

I returned to my car deeply humbled by the kindness she had afforded me in her darkest hour.

A few weeks before Wendy's deterioration, she imparted a little nugget of wisdom to me, and one that I shall never forget.

She told me that each day I wake up, I should have the mentality to discover what I can do for somebody else, and never to wake up expecting to discover what somebody might do for me.

That was the way Wendy had lived her Christian life for as long as she could remember. And it is one I shall endeavour to live out each day for the rest of my life.

What is it I can do today to help someone today?

In Wendy's final moments she did something for me that I will treasure forever. Is there anything you can do today to help someone, and something that person will treasure forever also?

Bishop Timothy Bavin
Anglican Bishop and Monk

Healthy kidneys require substantial liquid intake, although our bodies do not have an infinite capacity – as a vicar discovered one afternoon on his pastoral rounds. For in house after house he was offered and received a cup of tea, until he arrived – awash – at the last house on his list.

Again, the offer was made, and he would have declined it were it not that his refusal would have caused some offence. So, when presented with a steaming brew of Earl Grey in the finest bone china, he accepted.

However the phone rang and his hostess left the room to answer it, and he was able to look around for somewhere to tip the contents of his cup. But there were no flowers, pot plant, vase or even coal scuttle; so he opened the window and with great relief threw the brew into the garden.

As he did so, the cup came away from its handle, and at that moment his hostess returned to find him standing disconsolately with all that remained of a treasured piece of Worcester in his hand.

Because he had not faced and dealt with his problem at the beginning of his visit, he had hoped for the best, but with embarrassing consequences.

It reminds us that there is no substitute for immediate action when one is confronted by a serious issue, whether of health or anything else.

Dame Judi Dench
Actor
Always look for the plusses.

Juliet Nicolson
Writer and Journalist
"God grant me the serenity to accept the things I cannot change,
the courage to change the things I can
and the wisdom to know the difference."

Sometimes I recite the Serenity Prayer to myself a dozen times a day. These few lines have the capacity to identify almost every challenge I face, every decision I am confronted with.

By taking a moment of stillness to work out whether I can summon the courage to change something that is troubling me, or whether I should simply accept whatever it is, I find the reassurance and peace of mind that I am seeking.

I wish I had grown up knowing this prayer.

Rollo Armstrong
Music Producer and Founding Member of the band Faithless
Woody Allen said, "Ninety percent of success is just turning up."

In my business this has always felt true.

Talent alone is not enough. Rather, it is in the being there and staying there, being present, willing and able.

Often this is the major difference between those who should or could have done it and those who actually did it.

Dr Mya-Rose Craig
Ornithologist, Author and Campaigner for Equal Rights
It feels strange giving advice when I am only twenty years old, but I have thought of a few things. In 2022, my memoir, *Birdgirl*, was published, which is about growing up with my mum experiencing severe bipolar disorder and how going out into nature helped us cope as a family, despite the impact on my own mental health.

My advice is to enjoy every second of your time with your family.

I went on my first long-distance birding trip with my parents and older sister to South Africa when I was four years old. My dad drove us 10,000km in four weeks whilst I was sometimes a nuisance in the back. Despite this my sister and I bonded, and she says that taking me to see the African penguins on the beach, just the two of us, was one of the highlights of her life, as it is for me.

It is never too early to take your children on trips to engage with nature.

Stuart Pollard
Educator and Teacher

Learning about the social model of disability changed the way that I view teaching, learning, inclusion and schools. It affects my daily practice as an educator. Peter Mittler puts it far more clearly than I ever could: "Inclusion is not about placing children in mainstream schools. It is about changing schools to make them more responsive to the needs of all children."

All too often, I hear from and work with the parents of children excluded from schools, and I think that if Mittler's nugget was known, understood and applied more widely, this would not be the case.

Anthea Turner
Television Presenter

Self care isn't selfish.

I spend a lot of time talking to people who put themselves at the bottom of the self care list.

If you have trouble with this and feel guilty for doing something for yourself here's my advice.

How many people rely on your strength, health and ability to provide? I bet quite a few.

Think of your health as a bank of gold and as the years go by it increases in value, therefore it makes perfect sense to protect it so you can protect others.

You are precious, you are gold.

James Runcie
Novelist, Documentary Filmmaker, Television Producer and Playwright
Things I have learned:
Try not to worry about things you cannot control.
Keep your friendships in good repair.
Never insult your children.
Leave a place knowing you might always return to it.
Leave a person thinking you might never see them again.
Seize the day, remember well, love fiercely.

Andy Cole
Kidney recipient and ex Manchester United Football Player
As we know, it's not easy. Keep your head up, keep moving forward and surround yourself with positive people who want to see you better.

Rabbi Jonathan Wittenberg
Senior Rabbi of Masorti Judaism UK and Author
Maimonides, who was physician to the court of Saladin as well as arguably the greatest rabbi of the Middle Ages, draws on a seemingly unlikely source to underline the obligation to heal.

The Torah says that wherever possible lost property must be returned, and what greater possession can we lose than our health. Therefore, whoever endeavours to restore it to us performs the greatest of *mitzvot*.

That is why those who work for the health and wellbeing of society deserve our deepest gratitude and support.

Lynda La Plante CBE
Writer and Screen Writer
A long time ago I was playing Lydia Languish in the touring production of *The Rivals*. I had a very tight corset and a bustle. The weight of the gown, the heavy train balanced on the bustle, used to give me back ache. One night after feeling very unwell as if I had a slight temperature, the unusual relief of removing the costume, the corset and the weighted heavy bustle, I still felt excruciating

pain and it steadily got worse. In the middle of the night, I was found wandering the hotel corridor and collapsed. In the hospital I was diagnosed with acute inflammation of my kidneys and given antibiotics, and pain relief. It was discussed that I should be placed on standby in case I required dialysis.

I was very fortunate to be cured, but I have never forgotten the excruciating pain, and the incredible attention from the staff. I also met whilst in the ward many patients waiting for kidney transplants and others attending for their dialysis treatment. Although ever since that time, I have been more than aware of how precious kidneys are in the function of your body remaining healthy.

The Lady Judith Solomon Award Fund to drive improvements in dialysis, I hope gains momentum by a few nuggets from people like me who came so near to their dependency but also were made aware of the importance of expanding the research.

The weighty period costume however did not encourage me to end my acting career, being a full time writer has by far more benefits, physically at least.

Dame Jacqueline Wilson
Novelist

Have you ever read the classic children's book *Pollyanna* by Eleanor H Porter?

Pollyanna's father teaches her to try to look for a silver lining when life seems harsh by playing a Glad Game. This positive attitude can make people groan nowadays, and the Monty Python crew and their song "Always Look on the Bright Side of Life" lampoons the idea mercilessly and yet it can be surprisingly effective.

Scientific studies show that cardiac patients who try to be grateful for small things considerably improve their heart health. I've had heart failure myself and pertinently to this anthology I've had kidney failure too. (Trust me to be a diva and have two vital organ failures!) I was obviously worried during my descent down the various stages of kidney failure till I reached the alarmingly titled "end stage". My subsequent eighteen months on dialysis were a bit of a trial. Of course I didn't skip around singing "Glad that I Live am I."

However, I found it didn't help if I moaned and whined and felt sorry for myself. It worked better for me, and certainly my patient partner, if I tried to stay positive. When my kidneys could barely cope and I was starting to feel really ill it was good to know that I could start dialysis – simply because the alternative was much more grim! I chose to have haemodialysis, and it was a relief knowing there have been huge improvements in treatment over the years. Very few patients have to clutch those wretched grey sick bowls nowadays whilst on dialysis. No-one can actually enjoy having two big needles stuck in your arm and your body being turned into a bizarre washing machine, but the Filipino nurses were the sweetest, kindest, gentlest people I have ever met, and tried their hardest to make it less of an ordeal.

It's surprisingly bearable if you tuck into a one-handed picnic during the four hour process, and if you're a bookworm like me you can get through a lot of novels. I even dictated 100,000 words of one of my own children's books to my partner – I said she was patient. You can watch television if you wish, do a crossword, or have a doze. Dialysis doesn't have to disrupt your life. I stayed working hard, writing two books a year, and doing many events and book signings. I wasn't being courageous it was just my way of coping. I know it's much harder to stay working if you have a physically demanding job, though some valiant people manage to do this. It helps so much not to let your illness take over and define you as a person.

When you're on dialysis three times a week you can still go away on holiday. You can make a booking at dialysis units all over this country, and even abroad. I love going to north Norfolk so went to a brilliant unit there. I could have a morning on the beach or exploring, have my treatment in the afternoon, and then be free all evening to have a stroll in the sunset after supper. It's easy to play the Glad Game in those circumstances, though it's a struggle to be positive about meals.

I didn't realise how restricted a kidney patient's diet is before I became ill. All the things I love best – fruit, vegetables, coffee, chocolate, chips – are suddenly very bad for you, and salt is forbidden. It's a bland and boring diet no matter how hard you try to see the bright side, but you've got the incentive to stay as fit as possible so that you can be eligible for a transplant one day.

My partner and I aren't compatible where blood groups are concerned but due to a marvellous living kidney sharing system we eventually got lucky. I've now had my donated kidney for eight years and it's so easy to be gladly grateful for these extra marvellous years of productive life. And gladder still that Kidney Research UK are doing such amazing work. Let's hope that easier dialysis and transplant techniques are looming on the horizon. My dad had exactly the same heart and kidney failure that I've had and died when he was fifty-seven. I'm twenty years older than that, and fingers crossed I'm still going strong. I'm so grateful.

Imogen Stubbs
Actor and Writer
"Though much is taken
Much abides".
Alfred, Lord Tennyson.

Nina Nannar
Journalist
Never take each day for granted.

Claire Waxman OBE
Independent Victims' Commissioner for London
This quotation resonates with me, as my work is centred on giving a platform to voices that have been silenced or victimised: "Remaining silent in the face of an injustice perpetrates more injustice. Find the courage to speak out and make your voice heard".

Sathnam Sanghera
Journalist and Author
It's almost never about you.
When people criticise you in public, or praise you, what they have to say is almost always about them. It's often true in relationships and friendships too.

Elizabeth Day
Author and Broadcaster
Every failure contains within it something you can learn.

It might not be immediately apparent. It might take weeks, months or even years, but at some point, if you choose to, your understanding of life will be deeper because of it – even if the lesson is simply that you were able to survive.

The Very Revd Andrew Nunn
Former Dean of Southwark
"In everything do to others as you would have them do to you."
Matthew 7.12

It's not often that people from across the world, cultures, religions, time and place agree on anything but this is one thing that people have agreed on.

The Golden Rule, as it is most often called, can be found popping up all over the place, including in the Bible. It's simple, it's memorable, it's potentially life changing.

"Do to others as you would have them do to you."

Just imagine if we could actually live by this rule, if we did what it asks, if I lived like this, if my neighbour lived like this. It would be a world transformed.

The deep sadness is that we can't seem to do it but that shouldn't stop us wanting, striving, seeking to do it, to live by it.

"Do to others as you would have them do to you."

It's as golden and simple as that.

Her Honour Judge Dafna Spiro
Circuit Judge
Why would someone want to read my nugget because, after all, I am an imposter!

I cannot quite believe that I am a judge because sometimes I still feel like a teenager. Then, I look in the mirror and see that those days are well and truly gone but in place of youth is wisdom and experience.

I remind myself, "Be proud of who you are, Dafna, and what you have become but never forget where you have come from".

If you are true to yourself, maintain your integrity and stick to your values then you will neither be nor ever need to feel like an imposter. Don't give up on your dreams but don't be fixed in what those dreams are.

Life is a journey and whilst it is important to retain a vision of the lofty heights that you aspire to, it is more important to enjoy the sights and experiences along the way; and always make time for family and friends – there is nothing that matters more.

Suzie Miller
Playwright, Librettist and Screenwriter
"Fortune favours the bold" was my childhood mantra.

As a girl this meant simple things like diving into a terrifyingly wild Australian ocean, about venturing into bushlands where snakes and spiders lay in wait – each time knowing that if I survived I would feel strong, able, more connected to something outside my own self. But boldness has evolved for me as an adult. Now boldness is about trying to "take action", speak up, stand strong for who and what I believe in, and in doing so being prepared to take the sort of risks that have a whole different terror. The fortune one reaps is perhaps a life of true connection and passion.

As a kid who only dreamt of changing the world, becoming a human rights lawyer was a profession I cherished, loved. But as a storyteller, I always wanted a creative way to reach people, to start conversations outside courtrooms. My first play offered a human side of inequity, it ignited conversations amongst more people than I had been able to reach in years of legal work. This blew my mind. I knew then that I needed to live outside the legal system and make a difference by living my passion, giving words to feelings and speaking out. But how does this happen? How to leave behind a profession that had provided the structure for me to have my own voice, a sense of security, status even. I had not come from a family of university-educated people, and had worked so very hard to get here, to be good at it, to be accepted; surely I couldn't walk away from this – that wasn't courage surely that was pure craziness? But then, after a year of terrible illness from which I was lucky to recover, I saw up close how short life was, how quickly one can lose it. I needed to "do" those things I had always said "one day I will boldly do". It occurred to me that boldness is very aligned with the act of doing something now. Not waiting for the "right" time but choosing to jump into that terrifying ocean of unknown now. I recognised that for me, as an adult, boldness became about risking rejection; about wriggling free from the structures of law, its financial and intellectual security, and exposing my inner and creative self to the world. Courage is said to be about feeling the fear and boldly going there anyway. To dare to face the rejection of those you are close to, by those who have power over you or your career, by those who "warned you not to". In all it is to risk failure and shame. And yet, without risking all of this, there was no way to really reach out.

Boldness for me in my work is now about writing from a place of risk, a place of unknown. Writing through the paradoxes and knots of human frailty and systemic challenges.

In my personal life it is about speaking up in those awkward moments against casual racism, sexism, classism and that weird low-grade bullying that comes up without warning. It's about having a voice that isn't just against the easy targets but is in conversations that are anxiety-provoking; in conversations with people we are afraid to confront. It is about living one's values and passions and finding ways to talk about difficult things without alienating others. It's less about raging and more about practising and refining a language that can be heard, and that can effect real engagement and considered change. I admire people who do this without thinking, but I admire more those people who risk when they do so. Those are the bold people amongst us. Long may they reap the fortune of knowing they are choosing to live the values they hold dear; long may they reap the fortune of a life truly well lived.

May we all cherish those who live boldly and acknowledge the terror it has taken.

> **Always be true** and truthful to yourself.

Joan Armatrading CBE
Musician

Jeremy Connick
Business Builder

Amongst an ocean of joy, I have had two difficult periods in my life. I learnt a lot from the experiences and I'd like to share a nugget from each.

The first period of difficulty was just the consequence of a demanding job and an inability to balance the demands of that job with everything else in my life. So pretty much self inflicted and not exactly a novel issue. Kids, my wife, friends, sport and so on were all playing second fiddle to my job. The consequence of defaulting to work was that for the first time in my life and at the age of forty, I was unhappy. Outwardly I had everything – great job, amazing family and no worries – but somehow I just wasn't happy.

A wise friend made me realise that the aim of life is not perfection in one thing but balance across all the important parts of your life. I started to keep a score on a chart of how I felt I was performing across all those important elements of life and began to adjust my life to ensure that I didn't just default to work. I began to plan my life and do small stuff every day that made me happy.

One of the first things that I did was take an hour for breakfast with my wife after dropping the kids at school. The world didn't end. Nobody cared. For the two of us it was weirdly thrilling and all for the price of two coffees and two pastries.

I began to rely on others at work and just focussed on the bits of my job that I felt I was really good at and that freed up time for the rest of life. In a relatively short time, I was still giving myself a decent grade for my work performance, but in my weekly self review I was getting good marks for all the other important parts of my life. Slowly, the fog lifted and I was back to bouncing around and enjoying life. In taking control of my life and actively grading myself, I saw that little bits of time spent each day with loved ones or playing sport or doing the other things I loved were so much better than grand gestures or living for vacations, and for me that was a great lesson.

The second nugget I learnt after my first wife passed away.

She took her life in circumstances that I still can't comprehend. I was a broken human for a long time. She'd been my best friend, and without her I was completely lost.

I had our kids to look after and so a reason to get up and get moving, but as I looked forward to the rest of my life, all I could see was a dark and lonely tunnel. It was more than frightening. I was explaining this to one of my oldest (in both senses) friends and he thought for a while and then said to me, "Just let the future come to you".

Some people tell you not to worry about the future – but that's a subtly different concept that I struggle to implement. As a parent and an adult who has been on the receiving end of some trauma, it's hard to "not worry" even though the advice makes complete sense.

On the other hand letting the future come to me was and is something that I found easy. It's a passive thing. "Just go with life", is how I interpret it and because I had suffered loss, I realised that it was difficult to see another scenario coming along that could eclipse what I'd already suffered. So why not let life come to me and deal with the twists and turns as they occur?

This nugget helped me through and may be something useful in times of distress.

Jonathan Cohen
Pianist, Composer and Musical Director

Nearly ten years ago my mother died from Alzheimer's disease. I understand that tragedy affects us all at some point in our lives, and suffering is ever present to varying degrees. Music can be a balm and a friend.

I am wholly grateful to live a life in music and I find pleasure, comfort and healing in the act of music making. Great composers from centuries ago can reach across the divide of time and touch our lives to impart great wisdom and comfort. Love and compassion can shine through the ages in music.

Martin Luther: "My heart, which is so full to overflowing, has often been solaced and refreshed by music when sick and weary."

Wayne Marshall OBE
Pianist, Organist and Conductor
In the music business you never get a second chance to make a first impression.

Derren Brown
Illusionist, Mentalist and Writer
The greatest nugget is that life never reduces itself to nuggets.

The tidiness of a comfy maxim is always undermined by the mess of real life and its failure to slot in neatly alongside our demands. The only useful pearls of wisdom are those that allow us to live in easier accordance with that inconvenient fact.

So, we might decide that what lies outside of our control is fine, because we cannot change it anyway.

With a sense of relief and liberation, we might consider that despite all appearances, it is not the things in the world that cause our problems, but instead our reactions to those things and the stories we tell ourselves about them.

We might lower our expectations of the world because it owes us nothing, and is full of people as disappointing and hurtful as we are.

We might work on ourselves rather than expect others to work around our problems.

We could, when we remember, lean more into compassion and gratitude because they encourage the happiest repercussions in an often abrasive world.

When it comes to relationships, the quality of our friendships will be the most important thing to us when we're older so we might pay more attention to them in youth. And in romance, there is no-one quite right for us, because for our partner to not cause us pain, they would have to be a mere projection of our demands, which in turn amount to the prickly fallout of our muddled childhoods. They would not be equipped to save us from ourselves and the tyranny of those demands, which might be their true task. We can, instead, allow our partners to remain something of a mystery, someone we could spend a lifetime getting to know, and rather than seek to change them, pay attention to how they might change us.

Finally, forget self-esteem: if we can take some responsibility for ourselves, and pursue something meaningful amongst all the mess, we are doing more than well enough.

Keith Brymer Jones
Potter and Judge on The Great Pottery Throw Down
A relationship should be "twice as good, half as bad" – meaning, when you're with the right partner and things are good you have someone to share them with, and when things are bad, they are only half as bad as you have someone to support you.

When it's twice as bad and half as good – think about moving on.

Brian Cookson OBE
Former President of the Union Cycliste Internationale
The world is not changed by snarky comments on social media nor by whingeing or complaining with your mates. You have to make change happen. So if you aren't happy about something, if you want to change the world, or just change the bits of it that affect you, if you want to make something happen, then there is no point waiting for other people, you have to get involved and work to make that change happen.

Jill Allen-King OBE
Author and Pride of Britain Lifetime Achievement Award Winner
After going totally blind on my wedding day at the age of twenty four in 1964 I thought it was the end of my life.

I had my left eye removed just after my first birthday through measles but had lived a normal life, going to an ordinary school and college. I worked in London as a chef for seven years. I passed all my exams for ballroom and Latin American dancing. I ran a Girls Brigade company.

After having my daughter my life changed, so I had something to live for.

I had no rehabilitation and spent the first seven years housebound, only going out when my husband or parents took me out.

I started to campaign to improve services and facilities as well as access for guide dogs.

Over the years I have had so many friends who have suffered with all kinds of disabilities.

My best friend died of cancer at the age of thirty-eight and left her husband and three young children. This depressed me more than going blind.

Life is too short and we must use the time we have to do what we can to help each other.

Phyllida Law OBE
Actor
Never think further than dinner or tea.

Professor Sir Partha Dasgupta
Economist and Frank Ramsey Professor Emeritus of Economics at the University of Cambridge
Many, many years ago, I went into my father's study to ask him something. On seeing me he stopped his writing and said to me, almost in passing, that one should only judge persons of the past by how far they were able to rise above their natural gifts and their social environment. He said Gandhi was not born beautiful and was of only modest intellect and means, but by supreme moral perseverance became the Mahatma we all recognise in him. My father went on to say that it is petulant self-indulgence to criticise past societies for practising what we today see as wrongs. He said we would refrain from doing that if only we were to ask ourselves what future people might say of our own practices.

He thought we should instead get on with our lives and do the best we can for ourselves and others.

Susannah Constantine
Fashion Stylist, Television Presenter and Author
"Don't worry about the things you cannot change or those that haven't yet happened. We only have today".

William Roache OBE
Actor
Life is meant to be enjoyed but as the years move on everyone thinks of slowing down, others tend to do things for you and everyone assumes you are getting weaker and more helpless, so I make sure I don't slow down but continue to do what I enjoy in life.

If someone offers me a chair under the assumption that I might need one because I'm of a certain age, I say, "Thank you but standing is my exercise."

The power of the mind is incredible, so when I was seventy I decided to get younger every year, and I feel about fifty now but am actually ninety-one.

Do not give up anything because of age, and remember that enjoyment is the key.

Brian Viner
Journalist and Author
You never know what worse luck your bad luck has saved you from.

I wish I could claim that wonderful scrap of insight as my own, but actually it comes from Cormac McCarthy's brilliant 2005 novel, later turned into a superb film, *No Country For Old Men*. As a simple philosophical doctrine to help us all through life, it seems to me about perfect. There are lots of maxims that mean almost the same thing – every cloud has a silver lining, look on the bright side, make sure your glass is half-full, stuff like that – but none of them quite matches McCarthy's line, because it's such a comforting way to look at misfortune.

Sometimes, of course, we find out precisely what worse luck our bad luck has saved us from. I have a friend who in December

1988 had a wedding to attend in New York but was briefly hospitalised following a road accident in London on the day of his flight, forcing him to miss it. That was bad luck. The flight was Pan Am 103, which crashed over Lockerbie killing all 259 people on board, and 11 on the ground. That was worse luck.

I'm sure we can all think of less extreme examples of that bad luck/worse luck equation in our own lives, not to mention all those times when, true to the McCarthy aphorism, we just don't ever know. Either way, it's a great tip for dealing emotionally with adversity.

Needless to add, adversity comes in many forms. One person's major disaster might be a minor headache for someone else. Everything's relative, which brings me to my second nugget of wisdom, issued quite unintentionally by a little old lady crossing the road. It was years ago in West Palm Beach, Florida, and this lady was with her similarly ancient friend, who was shuffling across the road at the same kind of tortoise-speed, only very, very marginally quicker. As I passed them I heard the one who was half a pace behind call out in tremendous irritation: "Sylvia, for God's sake, I said walk, not run."

That's a worthwhile life lesson too. When you're ninety two, running doesn't mean the same thing as it does when you're twenty-nine. We'd all do well to remember that.

Mark Wigglesworth
Conductor and Writer
Everyone lies on a spectrum of self-confidence and insecurity. Though there are situations where we might benefit from a high degree of certainty and other times when circumspection is appropriate, a worthy goal is probably a healthy dose of both.

Musicians share their lives with some of the greatest achievements of human civilization. How is it possible not to feel insignificant alongside Bach's B Minor Mass or inadequate when looking at the score of Mozart's *The Marriage of Figaro*? We are not worthy so much as to gather up the semiquavers from the sketches of Schubert's table. And yet, composers expect performers of their works to have sufficient self-assurance to shed all personal inhibition and lay bare their souls to an audience of strangers in order that music can be heard with the passion and sincerity that comes from complete conviction.

You cannot be a musician without the confidence to believe you have a right to express the emotions of others. Yet without the humility to discover what those emotions really are, the result will always be more about you than about the music itself. It is then limited by that identity.

It is not just in your preparation that musicians have to ask questions. It is necessary in performance too. The most important thing a musician does is listen. Most music involves playing with others, and it is what your fellow performers do that constantly affects the musical choices you yourself make. The challenge of simultaneously listening and creating is what makes music such a fundamentally human activity. To listen to others is not to abdicate responsibility for your own opinion. It is not a sign of weakness to be open to alternatives. Music shows that leading and following need not be contradictions.

It can be a struggle to reconcile the need for both doubt and confidence. The secret, I suppose, is not to see them as opposites in the first place. To be or not to be need not be a binary choice. To be and not to be is perfectly valid. In fact it takes confidence to be vulnerable. And only by questioning ourselves can we find the best within us. Vulnerability is a strength and if one's self-confidence is so high that it precludes the opportunity for growth, then that is where the weakness lies. An artist without doubt is an artist with answers and an artist with answers is not asking the right questions. The most interesting questions have no answers. That is not as unsettling as it might sound. It simply acknowledges that the security that comes from certainty is merely an illusion.

Certainty does not really exist. Of that I am sure.

Professor Janet Lord CBE
Professor of Immune Cell Biology, University of Birmingham

I reached my early thirties overweight and unfit. I had never got involved in any form of exercise. I was a total couch potato.

One day I was in the park with my two year old and realised I simply could not run around without puffing and panting. So I decided there and then to try and get fit and lose weight.

As a working mum it had to be something I could do when and where I could. So I chose running. I bought some running shoes and did my first run, more of a trot, exactly one mile around the block where we lived. I had to stop four times and felt sick by the end. However I stuck with it and one year later I ran my first half marathon. I am now sixty-six, I still run every day and it helps me stay healthy, both physically and mentally.

Find some form of exercise that you enjoy and can do easily and even if at first it is hard, stick with it.

Simon Callow CBE
Actor

Learn to listen, really deeply, to your own thoughts. Practice makes perfect. Don't analyse your inner promptings: just act on them. You then have only yourself to blame, but at least you have remained true to yourself.

Adrian A McDowell
Chair of Cycling Without Age Scotland

When I was a young man my late dad used to buy me the *Reader's Digest*. There was always a contribution I looked forward to: "The most unforgettable person I have ever met." A few years ago I met such a person – Norman.

I chair a wonderful charity – Cycling Without Age Scotland – introduced to Scotland by our inspirational CEO Christine Bell. She brought two adapted trishaws from Denmark, where it all started, to take out people from care homes, those who live alone, or are lonely, so that they can feel the wind in their hair and remember that life is for living.

When I joined our Board of Trustees I was immediately struck by Norman's energy, enthusiasm, and the warmth of this sprightly man with a twinkle in his eye and a ready smile in his early eighties.

His humour and love of life was infectious – he enthused all those who were fortunate to make his acquaintance.

His energy was unbounding and he was not familiar with the word "No." He became known as Stormin' Norman.

He had moved to Perth and when he heard about CWAS he became involved – and even though already in his senior years he threw himself into developing this young organisation.

He knew how to persuade people to loosen the purse strings and help buy trishaws. He encouraged students from Perth High School together with the Guildry Incorporation of Perth to raise funds to purchase two. He loved life and he loved people. He dedicated his life to helping and serving others.

Sadly he passed away in April 2022.

I remember a few Christmases ago he chuckled as he gave me my present – it was a name plate bearing the words, Chairman of the Bored. Life was never boring when Norman was around.

We miss him terribly but he has left us with the wonderful memory of a man who gave his all.

We now have two trishaws amongst our stock of one hundred and sixteen that are named Mary, after his wife, and Stormin' Norman.

Happily, Norman's daughter Lorna is still involved with us and continues to help raise our profile.

Norman showed that enthusiasm for life and caring for people ripples outwards and makes the world a much better place.

Sema Gornall
Human Rights Activist and Social Entrepreneur, CEO of The Vavengers
Dear Girl Child,
You have been told time and time again that you have a certain role in this society. You are constantly being told your gender decides who you are supposed to be and what you are supposed to

do in this life. My nugget to you is: Don't listen to anyone who tries to place you in a box and keep you there.

Keep going, feel your feelings, and speak using your voice. You have a right to be yourself in this society and no one can define you but you. Don't give in to gender roles set out for you by others, no matter what you are told. You deserve the best of everything: success, happiness, freedom, wellness, friendship, a wealth of knowledge and education. You deserve to thrive as much as anyone else.

Girl child, only listen to what you want to do and who you want to be. Move forward no matter what you are told and what barriers are set against you. Just keep being you because you are perfect the way you are.

Know that by doing all of this, by standing up for yourself, you are showing the world your superpower.

Sam Blake
Writer

I found this quotation from French historian Lucien Febvre in the second-hand section of Waterstones in Gower Street when I was at university in London and it's stayed with me ever since.

Febvre said, "There are no necessities, but everywhere possibilities; and man, as a master of the possibilities, is the judge of their use."

Possibility is opportunity, and I've always believed that it's up to us to create our own opportunities from those possibilities. Whether that's trying to write a bestseller and find an agent, or get a bit of head space in a busy world.

I never see limits, only opportunities. Everything that I've built over the years has been a result of needing to make my writing better and passing on that experience and knowledge to help others succeed. Sometimes you have to pivot – not necessarily start again, but reorientate and look at something from a new angle, and think outside the box to make the most of the possibilities. But every challenge creates opportunity, no matter how difficult it seems. We only grow when we're outside our comfort zone.

The best advice I was ever given was by my author friend, Sarah Webb "just keep writing", and without a doubt Malcolm Gladwell's theory that you reach the tipping point of success after 10,000 hours of practice applies to writers too.

I also love Jim Rohn's idea that, "we are the average of the five people we spend the most time with."

My five people are important to me, but I talk to everyone, everywhere I go, whether it's on the train or at an event. I'm fascinated by people and their stories, and listening is 99% of that process. Every conversation is a learning opportunity, a chance for an idea to seed – everyone has a story.

My eighth bestseller has just been published, and stayed in the Irish top ten for seven weeks – this year my first YA novel *Something Terrible Happened Last Night* hits the shelves. It's only happened because I've created opportunities from the possibilities.

Nadiya Hussain MBE
Chef, Writer, Television Presenter and
Winner of The Great British Bake Off, 2015

We don't realise that we walk around with these teeny tiny nuggets of advice, words, golden shimmering pieces of wonder. We are filled to the brim with them, but we don't know it, because we don't believe that we have the power to make a difference. Well, that's not true at all.

I have accumulated a few in my years, through things that people have told me quietly in a crowded room, things I have to digest in anger and lessons I have learnt through my own journey.

Other people's words, their wisdom, become our words and they become the lessons we teach ourselves, strengthening our inner voice, so we can be the people we want to be.

Life is always going to challenge you, at every single turn. Just when you think it's safe to come out it will be there, ready with another challenge. Every single day you will feel it, big or small those challenges will be there. Some of those days you will feel like giving up.

But think about all of those times. You got up when you were tired. You made do when you had no money. You smiled when you were broken. You stood tall when you were frightened. When you had no one, you did it all alone.

Just remember that was all you. No one else. Just you.

There is strength in knowing your own strength.

Julie Siddiqi MBE
Founder, Together We Thrive

Watching and listening to news reports, the natural and usual optimism and hope in me can sometimes be challenged.

Divisive language from politicians, people arriving into our country being kept in inhumane conditions, tensions in communities, online spaces being used to spread hate and misogyny.

Or trust depleting in institutions like the police, being found to have too many in their ranks acting in ways that are completely inappropriate and unacceptable. Or the cost of living affecting some in profound and difficult ways while others exploit and use their power and influence to make more and more money on the back of others who are really struggling.

It can feel overwhelming and one can feel hopeless and left with a sense that the issues are too big for us to navigate or to do anything about.

I recently got back from my first ever visit to Israel and Palestine which had a profound impact on me. Places like Jerusalem and Bethlehem that I have heard about all of my life, I was now walking those streets. I was moved to tears many times, visiting holy sites, the depth and meaning was inspiring but also challenging. The beauty, the history, the spirituality, the creativity, the humanity. All alongside death, anger, destruction, confusion, dividing walls and binary narratives of hate and fear. The pull between religion and politics was palpable everywhere we went. For many, the physical security barriers make it impossible to meet "the other".

The Holy Land as we often like to call it didn't always feel very holy at all.

But around every corner we were also lucky to meet inspirational souls who have chosen to not perpetuate cycles of hatred, to see humanity in those who they have been taught to fear, to be in the messy, difficult but brave spaces. And similarly I am constantly inspired through the work I do here in the UK, with Muslim and Jewish women, or alongside survivors of terrorism. Or when I support Muslim women to use their voice and agency to tell their own stories, to push back, to thrive and not to allow themselves to be defined by lazy and harmful stereotypes.

In the Qur'an the most quoted verse used as a reminder of bringing communities together says; "We have made you into nations and tribes so you may know one another". But what does that word, "know" really mean and how does that play out in our lives today?

It's so often easier to stay in silos, to just listen to certain views, to believe the rhetoric, to demonise people, to spread hate through our actions and also through our inactions.

One of the people we met on our trip was an Israeli father whose fourteen year old daughter was killed by a Palestinian suicide bomber. He sat next to a Palestinian man whose child had been killed by an Israeli soldier; they have developed a beautiful bond and friendship. That Israeli father said, "often we carry fear of what peace might look like". It was profound for me to hear it from him in that moment.

Another person we met said, "you don't have to be wrong for me to be right".

Because trying to see another opinion, challenging our own views, meeting people different from us, getting to know what makes someone tick and walking in their shoes, that is hard, it's messy, it can challenge us to the core. There are communities of people in our country who have genuine concerns for how their towns are changing. I feel we need to really listen to their fears and help them unpick those with patience and empathy, not with more labels and stereotypes.

So yes, my optimism is shaky at times but seeing real

peacemakers in action both here and abroad keeps my hope alive and gives me the lift I need to keep on going, even when it feels it may be easier to look, or walk, the other way.

Mark Beaumont
Long Distance Cyclist (World Record for a Circumnavigational Bike Tour of the World), Broadcaster and Author
The great, late BBC cameraman David Peat said to me when I was twenty-three years old when I was cycling around the world for the first time, "In life, aim to be valued for who you are, not for what you do."

At the time this made little sense, but as the years have passed I have held onto this. Lots of people have the same job title, have the same knowledge and skill, but you value people because of their character, their behavioural change under pressure, their humanity.

In terms of mental health and sense of worth, it's important to see yourself and others for who they are, not what they do for a job.

Angela Watt
Retired Renal Nurse
Anyone with chronic kidney disease knows that the future is uncertain, even if they are lucky enough to receive a transplant so my advice would be to always grasp the opportunities whenever they present and never just think "I can do that another time".

Marco Laurence
Entrepreneur and Philanthropist
"Prima il dovere, poi il piacere" is forever embedded in my mind. My nonno (grandfather), Roberto Hodara Z'L, taught me this repeatedly until it became part of my character.

The proverb translates to: "First duty, and then pleasure". Nonno's life epitomised this, viewing any material gain as an opportunity to help those less fortunate, but more importantly, ensuring that kindness was a priority rather than an afterthought.

Roberto's life was one of defiance and morality.

Hiding from the Nazis in the Dolomites, he had to confront the German army when they took up residence in the place he was lodging. Pretending to be part of the Portuguese Consulate, he and his family escaped from the hands of death and made their way to Italy.

Without a penny to his name, he began selling tools from a magazine. Still, he gave a portion of everything he earned to charity. His determination and entrepreneurial ability led to his creation of the largest tools distributor in Milan.

It is testament to his character that since his passing, some of his incredible deeds have been revealed by those he helped. He was described by a beneficiary as "the one man who never said 'no' in the forty years that I knew him".

Nonno was largely the inspiration behind my creation of The Warehouse – a non-profit designed to empower the Jewish community in the face of rising anti-semitism. We equip all our members (any race, colour or creed is welcomed) with the physical and mental tools to confidently navigate their lives. Since launching one year ago, we have helped over 5,000 individuals.

I am now embarking on a journey to create the latest world-changing tech company. I decided to first create a non-profit because: prima il dovere, poi il piacere.

I structure my days in a similar fashion; my mornings are the times where I pray, meditate, work out and journal, whereas my evenings are a time to relax and socialise.

Our duties are numerous, but I think of them in three categories of relationships: you and yourself; you and others; you and your maker. Each of these require delicate care and attention. Discovering who you want to be (rather than what you want to do) will make the exercise significantly easier.

If I can share one piece of wisdom which has truly changed my life, it is to focus on your duties before pleasure – prima il dovere, poi il piacere.

Sandra Currie
Chief Executive of Kidney Research UK

When I was a new student mental health nurse a rather scary Charge nurse who I worked with always said he "expected perfection from us because then he might get near to excellence", this led to us doing our very best to get as close to his perfection as possible and I am sure it increased our overall standards. I still strive for perfection when I can even although it won't be possible, but it keeps my expectations of myself high.

Another quote that I know has helped me in many challenging periods of life both professionally and personally is from Marie Curie, she said "nothing in life is to be feared, it is only to be understood. Now is the time to understand more, so that we may fear less."

Alexander Murphy
Speechwriter

I never enjoyed the pleasure or the honour of meeting Judith Solomon. I knew her only through my good friend, her daughter Juliet, and what she has told me about her. About her qualities of kindness, compassion and the quiet wisdom that inspired this book.

I lost my dear dad, Richard Patrick Murphy, about the same time Juliet lost Judith, and we walked through that long, dark, valley of grief together. We still walk it, helping each other as best we can.

Just as Judith was for Juliet, Richard was my greatest source of wisdom.

Richard was a man of infinite knowledge – a walking Wikipedia and a human Google long before the web was invented. He was a self-taught polymath whose mind teemed with history, politics, films, football, literature and more. Yet despite the thousands of books he imbibed he remained a man of few words.

By inclination and upbringing he wasn't prone to over-share. He was a son of the Liverpool-Irish working class, raised in wartime, learning to read in bomb shelters while the Luftwaffe drowned Bootle in a sea of fire yards above his head. His university was the long dock strikes which kept his own dad at home for long, hungry months, and his own early working life rolling barrels around a rum warehouse. So not for him any pompous proselytising, handing down Rules for Life as though they were chiselled in tablets of stone.

He was about "show" not "tell", and he shared his wisdom by example – living a life of honesty, decency and with a never-ending curiosity to understand the world better, which endured through to his final days.

The last book, unfinished at his bedside, was a doorstep history of Jerusalem.

He was reading it because "he didn't know enough about the Middle East." He was 83.

I remember only three nuggets of specific wisdom:
1. Never play a square pass across your own penalty area
2. Never wear brown shoes with a blue suit
3. Never tie your shoelaces in a revolving door

Time hasn't been kind to these.

He was aghast at the modern habit of defenders and goalkeepers playing pat-ball at the back.

I often twin tan brogues with a navy suit. No-one ever looks surprised.

Only the third holds good, you suppose.

So not much of a legacy in terms of formal advice. But that was the thing with Dad's wisdom, and the same is true with nuggets.

It was always there, just under the surface if you wanted to look, waiting to be treasured.

Sir Simon Schama
Historian

The last thing my father said to me before he died (in 1978) was "be brave". But he'd been giving me that advice since I was a small boy. He didn't mean it physically: climb a mountain or knock down a bully: but in the choice of life-work and the *way* one worked at it. He suffered from remorse for not defying his own father who, when told that theatre was how he wanted to spend his life, replied "Fine but don't ever come home again." So bravery for my dad was taking the plunge into work about which one was passionately engaged, that said something about the human condition and that connected with all kinds of people.

The call to creative bravery also meant not following the herd; not playing it safe; being open to hunches and surprises; going down a winding path; making the improbable seem suddenly essential. Take those chances; follow the instinct for freshness, originality, a new angle of things, and – as I have happily found – the rewards will come back to you, not the least of which will be personal happiness and a sense that, given we have just one go at life (as far as I know) we've given it all we've got.

Danny Brocklehurst
Screenwriter and Playwright
We are all faced with a series of opportunities brilliantly disguised as impossible situations.

Dame Zandra Rhodes
Fashion and Textile Designer
My nugget of wisdom would be: *don't let anything crush you*.

When I first started the Zandra Rhodes brand in 1969 I was told my designs were too 'extreme' for clothing. It took a trip to the USA to finally get my designs noticed and in-front of the High Priestess of American Vogue, Diana Vreeland. Diana put the Zandra Rhodes pieces on Natalie Wood and the rest is history! Always stay true to your authentic self, it will work out in the end.

Henning Wehn
Comedian
I will let you in on my one and only New Year's resolution, which I repeat every year.

"Don't get a heart attack."

Or as my old maths teacher, Herr Bratfisch, said when asked why he wasn't working in the potentially even more lucrative* private sector, "If you regularly have to go to your maximum, you're in the wrong job."

*Teaching in Germany is a cushy job with a big pension and a good salary, and, in my and Herr Bratfisch's day, school was out no later than 1.30 p.m.

Alan Titchmarsh MBE
Gardener and Broadcaster
To take your job seriously is imperative; to take yourself seriously is disastrous.

> **At the end of the game** the king and the pawn go back in the same box.
>
> *Italian proverb*

Juliet Solomon
Compiler of 'The Book of Nuggets'

Index of Contributors

A

Russ Abbot	*171*
Stig Abell	*180*
Michael Adams	*28*
Dr Maggie Aderin-Pocock	*184*
Ama Agbeze	*46*
Andy Airey	*164*
Professor Jim Al-Khalili	*127*
Rob Allen	*51*
Jill Allen-King	*212*
Tejal Amin	*33*
Professor James Appleby	*134*
Professor Jason Arday	*25*
Joan Armatrading	*208*
Rollo Armstrong	*199*
John Arnold	*67*
Leslie Ash	*56*
The Lord Austin of Dudley	*184*

B

Steve Backshall	*31*
David Baddiel	*24*
Annette Badland	*182*
David Bailey	*79*
Michael Ball	*85*
Peter Barker	*87*
Nigel Barley	*98*
Patrick Barrie (and Matthew Rose)	*27*
Sebastian Barry	*102*
Arthur Barzey	*69*
Dame Shirley Bassey	*109*
Stephen Bate	*178*
Bishop Timothy Bavin	*198*
Professor Sallie Baxendale	*174*
Dr Paul Baylis	*169*
Richard Beard	*105*
Mark Beaumont	*223*

Sir Anthony Beevor	*170*
Jonny Benjamin	*31*
Professor Richard Bentall	*118*
Christopher Biggins	*162*
Anne Mayer Bird (and Catherine Mayer)	*149*
Dickie Bird	*155*
Malorie Blackman (and Sir Derek Jacobi)	*185*
Sam Blake	*219*
Alison Bloxham	*134*
Dr Amra Bone	*19*
Sir Chris Bonington	*3*
Michael Booth	*118*
Sir Geoffrey Boycott	*12*
Martyn Brabbins	*107*
David Brabham	*163*
Sir Rodric Braithwaite	*168*
Jo Brand	*172*
Gyles Brandreth	*179*
Mike Brearley	*61*
Emma Bridgewater	*63*
Danny Brocklehurst	*227*
Professor Karim Brohi	*191*
Peter Brookes	*110*
Derren Brown	*211*
Steven Brown	*7*
Oliver Burkeman	*155*
Paul Burston	*64*
Dame Darcey Bussell	*175*

C

Simon Calder	*39*
Simon Callow	*217*
Alastair Campbell	*68*
Lucy Campbell	*36*
Lord Carlile of Berriew	*76*
Robert Carlyle	*1*
Jasper Carrott	*97*
Jim Carter	*149*
Jules Chappell	*86*

Debbie Chazen	*193*
The Hon. Mrs Justice Cheema-Grubb	*192*
Sheila Coates	*90*
Jonathan Cohen	*210*
Sir Ronald Cohen	*69*
Andy Cole	*201*
Jeremy Connick	*209*
Susannah Constantine	*214*
Tom Conti	*80*
Brian Cookson	*212*
Wendy Cope	*23*
Giles Coren	*121*
Cathy Courtney	*183*
Brian Cox	*155*
Rachel Cox	*71*
Sara Cox	*156*
Dr Mya-Rose Craig	*199*
Professor David Crystal	*2*
Professor Sir John Cunningham	*189*
Sandra Currie	*225*

D

Ann Daniels	*36*
Karen Darke	*68*
Professor Sir Partha Dasgupta	*213*
Gary Davies	*158*
Sir Ray Davies	*9*
Sharron Davies	*186*
Evan Davis	*144*
Elizabeth Day	*205*
Professor Clare Finburgh Delijani	*196*
Dame Judi Dench	*199*
Hugh Dennis	*175*
Amy Denny	*62*
Victoria Derbyshire	*120*
The Rt Hon. Lord Navnit Dholakia	*33*
Henry Dimbleby	*161*
Jonathan Dimbleby	*131*

Dr Jim Down	*129*
Drug Addicts Anonymous UK	*82*
Richard Dunwoody	*192*
Geoff Dyer	*21*

E

Professor Lucy Easthope	*106*
Jenny Eclair	*143*
Lily Ebert	*128*
Sir Mark Elder	*25*
Mark Emmerson	*111*
Matthew Engel	*34*
Sir Richard Evans	*84*
Simon Evans	*196*

F

Sebastian Faulks	*129*
Pam Ferris	*98*
The Lord Finkelstein	*27*
Cal Flyn	*193*
The Lord Foster of Thames Bank	*167*
Sir Brendan Foster	*130*
Tracy Foster	*85*
Michael Frayn	*82*
Jonathan Freedland	*71*
Dawn French	*14*
Alex Frost	*197*
Stephen Fry	*2*

G

Graeme Garden	*134*
Val Garland	*137*
Jane Garvey	*171*
Mel Giedroyc	*112*
Dr Shelley Gilbert	*122*
Tania Gilbert	*59*
Dame Evelyn Glennie	*106*
Sema Gornall	*218*

Matthew Gould — 99
David Gower — 185
Dame Katherine Grainger — 56
Jane Green — 143
Professor Baroness Susan Greenfield — 53
Abdulrazak Gurnah — 33

H

Brad Hall — 124
Sarah Hall — 80
Laurence Halsted — 160
Areeba Hamid (and Will McCallum) — 113
Janice Hamilton — 51
Sophie Hannah — 74
Thomas Harding — 103
Sir David Hare — 68
Joanne Harris — 56
Miranda Hart — 109
Sir Max Hastings — 98
Anne Hegerty — 113
Paul Henderson — 122
The Rt Hon. Lord Heseltine — 137
Ashley Hickson-Lovence — 81
Harry Hill — 102
Eileen Hogan — 183
Jools Holland — 125
Sir Stephen Hough — 189
Steph Houghton — 116
Lady Sarra and Sir Chris Hoy — 18
Professor Jeremy Hughes — 46
Gloria Hunniford — 114
Dr Musharraf Hussain — 140
Nadiya Hussain — 220
Corrine Hutton — 186
Neil Hyman — 4

I

Robin Ince — 15

John Inverdale	*186*
Jeremy Irons	*193*
Jack Isaac	*145*
Steven Isserlis	*97*

J

Sir Derek Jacobi (and Malorie Blackman)	*185*
Rhys James	*189*
Sir David Jason	*9*
Jonathan Jenkins	*54*
Professor Jagbir Jhutti-Johal	*26*
Alan Johnson	*11*
Dom Joly	*101*
Keith Brymer Jones	*212*
Griff Rhys Jones	*147*
Selwyn Jones	*14*
Judith	*135*

K

The Lord Kestenbaum	*173*
Her Honour Judge Judy Khan	*69*
Sadiq Khan	*13*
Roger Kirby	*157*
Vanessa Kirby	*154*
Nick Knowles	*181*
David Kynaston	*103*

L

Randeep Singh Lall	*148*
Bonnie Langford	*181*
Lynda La Plante	*201*
Marco Laurence	*223*
Phyllida Law	*213*
Professor John Paul Leach	*167*
Kim Leadbeater	*194*
Helen Lederer	*182*
Keith Leslie	*99*
Amanda Levete	*63*

Professor Liz Lightstone	*62*
Dame Maureen Lipman	*9*
Most Reverend Bernard Longley	*112*
Professor Janet Lord	*217*
Tim Lott	*106*
Dame Joanna Lumley	*180*
Linda Lusardi	*39*
Vijay Luthra	*22*

M

Iain Mackenzie	*41*
Sir Cameron Mackintosh	*172*
Rhian Mannings	*159*
Suhaiymah Manzoor-Khan	*103*
Professor Dame Sally Mapstone	*116*
Professor Sir Michael Marmont	*166*
Wayne Marshall	*211*
Catherine Mayer (and Anne Mayer Bird)	*149*
Kevin Maynard	*56*
Dr Barney McAweaney	*28*
Will McCallum (and Areeba Hamid)	*113*
Chris McCausland	*20*
Steve McClure	*138*
Vicky McClure	*82*
Robert McCrum	*51*
Adrian McDowell	*217*
Debbie McGee	*181*
Roger McGough	*100*
Duke McKenzie	*133*
Siobhán McSweeney	*181*
Oliver McTernan	*184*
Chris Mears	*122*
Jed Mercurio	*102*
Suzie Miller	*206*
Chief Rabbi Sir Ephraim Mirvis	*187*
Dr Sophie Mitchinson	*74*
Zara Mohammed	*22*
George Monbiot	*178*

Dame Clare Moriarty	*23*
John Motson	*171*
Harry Mount	*147*
Tony Mowbray	*165*
Etta Murfitt	*137*
Alexander Murphy	*225*
Figen Murray	*29*
Dame Jenni Murray	*95*

N

Nina Nannar	*205*
Zoe Newnham	*79*
Cardinal Vincent Nichols	*72*
Juliet Nicolson	*199*
Hermione Norris	*70*
Andrew Nunn	*205*
Professor Chi-chi Nwanoku	*58*

O

Tracy-Ann Oberman	*31*
Ed O'Brien	*3*
Francis O'Gorman	*16*
Jemima Olchawski	*168*
Mark Ormrod	*174*
Professor Olivette Otele	*150*
Nicholas Owen	*142*
Tim Owen	*164*
David Oyelowo	*101*

P

Elaine Paige	*111*
Sir Michael Palin	*4*
Mike Palmer	*165*
Matthew Parris	*93*
David Peace	*151*
Jonathan Pearce	*138*
Simon Pegg	*36*
Dr Max Pemberton	*157*

Alistair Petrie	*57*
Sir Trevor Phillips	*85*
Richard Pitman	*187*
Nigel Planer	*104*
Stuart Pollard	*200*
Su Pollard	*28*
Dr Kingsley Poole	*185*
Dr Mark Porter	*100*
Toby Porter	*133*
Sir Philip Pullman	*16*
Steve Punt	*137*

Q

Liam Quinn	*65*
Pauline Quirke	*47*

R

Monisha Rajesh	*237*
Adil Ray	*38*
Harry Redknapp	*52*
Amanda Redman	*115*
Dennis Reed	*154*
Samantha Renke	*146*
Dr Ben Reynolds	*171*
Dame Zandra Rhodes	*227*
Emma Rice	*141*
John Richards	*141*
Andy Riley	*136*
Robert Rinder	*173*
William Roache	*214*
Claudia Roden	*53*
Helen Rogerson	*191*
Lady Justice Rose	*33*
Matthew Rose (and Patrick Barrie)	*27*
Michael Rosen	*96*
Gaby Roslin	*138*
Nick Ross	*64*
James Runcie	*201*

Dr Malcolm Q Russell | *53*

S

Julia Samuel	*121*
Philippe Sands	*146*
Sathnam Sanghera	*204*
Dr Alastair Santhouse	*151*
Professor Marcus du Sautoy	*115*
Sir Simon Schama	*226*
Ashley Scott	*163*
Danny Sebastian	*142*
Sir Anthony Seldon	*97*
Professor Anil Seth	*84*
Katy Sexton	*31*
Dr Adnan Sharif	*65*
Dr Martin Shaw	*147*
Dharmesh Sheth	*146*
Professor Simon Shorvon	*126*
Julie Siddiqi	*221*
William Sieghart	*187*
The Rt Hon. Lady Justice Simler	*186*
Francesca Simon	*119*
Jasvir Singh	*115*
Ali Smith	*101*
Delia Smith	*11*
Karen Snell	*42*
Rian Snell	*43*
Dan Snow	*154*
Ben Soames	*162*
Zeb Soanes	*195*
Her Honour Judge Dafna Spiro	*205*
Professor Amia Srinivasan	*138*
Laura Stamp	*21*
Alison Steadman	*192*
Juliet Stevenson	*83*
Professor Chris Stringer	*149*
Imogen Stubbs	*204*
Zoe Sugg	*166*

Pandora Sykes *192*

T
Chris Tarrant *117*
Joelle Taylor *53*
Owen Teale *190*
Sophie Tebbetts *20*
Colin Thackery *145*
Christopher Timothy *161*
Alan Titchmarsh *228*
David Tovey *93*
Dr Chris Van Tulleken *179*
Anthea Turner *200*

V
Emilie Vanpoperinghe *95*
Salley Vickers *78*
Michael Vincent *35*
Jeremy Vine *170*
Tim Vine *38*
Brian Viner *214*
John Volanthen *175*

W
Nina Wadia *135*
Sir Terry Waite *6*
Dr Gee Walker *132*
Marjorie Wallace *88*
Sir Peter Wanless *177*
Maddy Warren *187*
Christie Watson *92*
Angela Watt *223*
Claire Waxman *204*
Justin Webb *128*
Henning Wehn *227*
Alison Weir *173*
Denise Welch *148*
Chrissie Wellington *153*

Professor Stephen Westaby *48*
Sara Wheeler *39*
Josh Widdicombe *36*
Mark Wigglesworth *215*
Toyah Willcox *104*
Yvette Williams *152*
Anna Williamson *120*
Dame Jacqueline Wilson *202*
Mark Wilson *40*
Jamie Windust *66*
Tim Winter *126*
Debbie Wiseman *182*
Rabbi Jonathan Wittenberg *201*
Judy Ling Wong *102*

z

Benjamin Zand *75*
Benjamin Zephaniah *34*

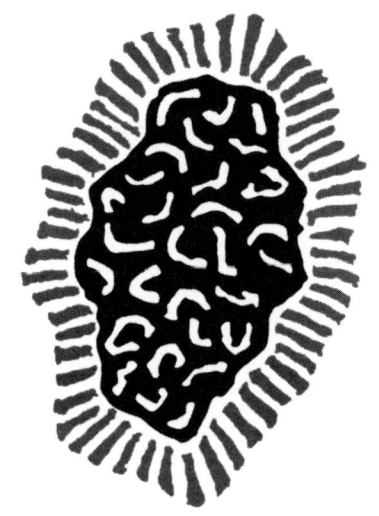

All the proceeds from the sale of this book
will go to Kidney Research UK